YOUR SEXUAL DREAMS INTERPRETED

YOUR SEXUAL DREAMS INTERPRETED

Pamela Ball

Capella

This edition published in 2006
by Arcturus Publishing Limited
26/27 Bickels Yard,
151–153 Bermondsey Street,
London SE1 3HA

Copyright © 2002 Arcturus Publishing Limited

All rights reserved. No part of this publication
may be reproduced, stored in a retrieval system,
or transmitted, in any form or by any means,
electronic, mechanical, photocopying, recording
or otherwise, without written permission in
accordance with the provisions of the Copyright
Act 1956 (as amended). Any person or persons
who do any unauthorised act in relation to this
publication may be liable to criminal prosecution
and civil claims for damages.

ISBN-13: 978-1-90032-26-1
ISBN-10: 1-900032-26-0

Cover design by Emma Haywood

Printed in England

CONTENTS

Introduction   7

SECTION ONE   10
The Way We See Ourselves   13
Relationships   17
Madonna v Whore and
Hero v Villain   25
Teenage Dreams   29
Homosexuality   34
Deviations   38
Fantasies   44

SECTION TWO
Sexual Symbolism   48

A-Z   49

SECTION THREE
Dream Interpretation   112

YOUR SEXUAL DREAMS AND FANTASIES EXPLAINED

INTRODUCTION

This book is primarily a workbook to enable dreamers to enhance their own lives through an understanding of their sexual dreams. While being a dictionary of symbols and information, it is also a practical handbook for future use and thought. It shows how a child develops, how attitudes arise, why we have sexual dreams and, finally, how to use sexual dreams constructively. It has been fun to write and hopefully will be fun to read.

The main focus of my work - and my own personal growth - has been the very delicate balance between masculinity and femininity both internally and externally, overtly and covertly, physically and spiritually. I have learnt, in part, to understand sexuality and have, using knowledge of dreams and symbolism, tried to achieve for myself the integration of the two sides of my personality without harming anyone else in the process. This book, while based on sound common sense and not just theory, also gives explanations on the need for wholeness through partnership we all have as part of our make-up (We are continually attempting to become a unified whole, while still being aware of an inner duality).

There is a basic story told in slightly different terms in most, if not all, religions, which highlights the interplay between the negative and positive aspects of the masculine and feminine, and between the spiritual and instinctual. It could be said that it is the essential plot - in one form or another - for all sexual dreams. You, the dreamer, will adapt the play to express yourself as freely as you can, and the more you know the more freely you can express yourself.

So, a slightly humorous telling of this tale is as follows:-
In the beginning there was Adam and his woman - her name was

Lilith. Lilith was a moody young madam who wouldn't always do as she was told. She was quite sensitive really, and didn't like it when Adam had better things to do. She used to get quite destructive, until it got to the point where Adam couldn't handle her and all he wanted was peace and quiet. He only wanted time to have long philosophical conversations with his friend God. She got annoyed when he did that, because she seemed to know all about what they talked about anyway. Adam sometimes felt lonely and also wanted to be looked after, but Lilith had got bored waiting and had gone off down to the lake to do her own thing there. She was making demons, all by herself!!!!! God then made Adam another woman because he was lonely. Her name was Eve. The problem was that she wanted him to do something he knew he shouldn't be doing and it was all going wrong again. Maybe he would have been better off sticking with Lilith in the first place. She was nice and sexy and she made him feel good all over.

The images which come up in dreams are drawn from personal experience, the unconscious self, and what Jung called the Collective Unconscious. Often when we are aware of the types of conflict within ourselves mentioned in the above story, we may dream in pairs (e.g. masculine/feminine, old/young, clever/stupid). An internal pendulum, which starts off swinging rather wildly from side to side, eventually comes to rest. It has compared and contrasted all the information it has collected along the way, and eventually sorts out the opposites into something which makes sense (A dream clarifying the masculine side of ourselves may be followed by a dream clarifying the feminine). The juggling that goes on in this way can take place over a period of time.

This book is divided into three sections:-
The first is an explanation of the various stages a human being may go through as he or she matures into a sexually competent person. These may include psychological concepts, actions or examples which are recognisable in everyday life.
The second section is an alphabetical listing of symbols, objects and ideas connected with sex and sexuality. Often the dreamer's

Introduction

mind will present things in symbolic form in order that the deeper meanings of the symbolism can be appreciated.
The third section is a number of case studies with interpretations at various levels of awareness to help readers eventually to interpret their own sexual dreams.

The easiest way to use this book is in conjunction with a good dream interpretation book, such as the author's own '10,000 Dreams Interpreted', and to write down the meanings gleaned to give the most effective interpretation. Using this book on its own will give the dreamer some basic explanations to enable him or her to understand how dreams can help us to deal with issues of relationship and sexuality.

SECTION ONE

The desire for union with someone else arises out of the appreciation that that person can give us feelings and experiences which we are unable to achieve in any other way. It often seems that we have lost a part of ourselves that only the other person can supply. Indeed, if all the various parts of us were fully integrated, we would not need to seek reassurance, confirmation of our attractiveness or love from others. Most of us have the desire either to become part of a greater whole or to make others part of us. Dreams with a sexual content or those about our sexuality provide the information to enable us to understand and eventually satisfy our needs. Sexuality and actions connected with sexual activity can make themselves apparent in various ways in dreams.

When a child is first born, it has to learn that it is now separate from its mother. It must cope with that separation - it begins to become 'conscious' of itself as a physical being, and of its need for warmth, comfort and love. The first stage of growth is the baby's fascination with its own body and its ability to be physical. This is as much to do with what feels comfortable and nice - how it feels to be in one's own skin, as it were. It is at this point that he or she learns about touch - whether it is nice to touch or be touched, and even if touch is permissible. If, for instance, the child is handled roughly a fear of being touched may develop which could later manifest as a sexual difficulty. While the original trauma may be suppressed, it will often surface in dreams when the time is appropriate. Real growth takes place when the individual is not afraid of the curiosity which allows an innocent exploration of his own body. Dreams will often allow us to explore this physicality in a safe way.

Moving on to more psychological aspects, we each hold within ourselves basic pictures - or concepts - of what masculine and feminine should be. These pictures are often distorted by our childhood experiences, that which we learn from the adults around us, and a growing perception of what is good and bad (or rather, right or wrong). The human being needs to know that it is 'right'. That does not necessarily mean gaining approval; it means more what feels right - a gut feeling.

C. G. Jung and his pupils made extensive studies of adults' perception of these basic concepts and were able to divide them into functions of thinking, feeling, sensation and intuition. It became possible to build up a type of 'map' of the interaction among all of these functions and to discover where one's own distortions occur.

Each function has a 'greater' and 'lesser' quality which it is possible to perceive as a separate personality or archetype. Each of the masculine and feminine sides of the personality has these four functions: thus there are 64 (8 x 8) connections possible. When our perception becomes twisted, we project onto those around us - or into our dreams - the archetype with which we have most difficulty. Our dreams will present us again and again with our own distortion, or we will have a tendency to repeat certain patterns of relationship over and over again. Until we learn how to cope with - and understand - our own distortion we can find ourselves in unsuitable relationships, such as a father/daughter type or a hero/princess. The other side of the coin is that, with awareness, one is able to accept others' projections onto oneself without being affected by them. Often in dreams the situations which need working through can manifest with a sexual bias in order for us to perceive the problem clearly.

The table below demonstrates the principle more clearly, and the archetypes are dealt with more extensively under the sub-heading 'People in Dreams' in the alphabetical section.

Your Sexual Dreams Interpreted

MALE	FEMALE	POSITIVE/ NEGATIVE	FUNCTION
KINDLY FATHER	KINDLY MOTHER	+	SENSATION
OGRE	DESTRUCTIVE MOTHER	-	
YOUTH	PRINCESS	+	FEELING
TRAMP	SIREN	-	
HERO	AMAZON	+	THINKING
VILLAIN	COMPETITOR	-	
PRIEST	PRIESTESS	+	INTUITION
SORCERER	WITCH	-	

Kindly Father and Mother are self-explanatory. Ogre represents masculine anger used negatively and Destructive Mother may be wilfully destructive, or simply the smothering type - that is, the mother who prevents the adequate growth of her children. Youth and Princess are the more gentle, fun-loving aspects of the personality, while Tramp is the eternal wanderer and Siren is the seductress or sexually active part of femininity. Hero is the self-sufficient Messianic part of the personality, while Amazon is the 'self-sufficient' female - the efficient businesswoman type. Villain is the masculine part of the self who uses power for his own ends. Competitor is the typical 'women's libber' who feels that she has no need for men. Priest and Priestess are the powers of intuition used for the 'greater good', while Sorcerer uses inner power totally dispassionately and Witch uses that same power rather more emotionally and perhaps negatively.

Perfect balance would be achieved by being able to use all these aspects of the personality in as constructive a way as possible. It would mean handling the negative, more difficult sides effectively, although not necessarily eradicating them.

THE WAY WE SEE OURSELVES

If we are going to understand what relevance the way we see ourselves - or rather the way we understand ourselves to be - has in dealing with our sexuality and sensuality, we need to comprehend how that self-image grows as we mature. It has been discovered that men's brains are different to women's - something that women have always known and appreciated anyway. Men's approach is almost always more logical and one-pointed than women's, which tends to be more dispersed and diffused.

The old idea that a person dreams him or herself into existence perhaps has foundation in fact. It is now accepted that a baby is aware before birth of what is happening 'on the outside'. There are also periods when what is called Rapid Eye Movement occurs in the foetus (Rapid Eye Movement is known to occur in a sleeping person when dreaming occurs). Thus the baby begins to internalise certain reactions to external stimuli and to respond accordingly.

We also know that the foetus is female for the first seven weeks in the womb. From that point on, there are those who will release a large quantity of the male hormone testosterone and will develop masculine characteristics, while others remain (and develop fully) as females. The brain develops in two halves; the left side of the brain is used for verbal and intuitive awareness and the right for spatial awareness and logical thought. These two halves are joined by something called the corpus callosum. This acts as a bridge between the two halves. It appears that although men's brains are some 10% bigger than women's, women are more efficiently 'wired' to be aware of what is going on. Women tend to use both sides of the brain in unison more effectively than men, and research is tending to reveal that women develop the 'bridge' to a greater extent. This is now beginning to change as men develop their intuitive abilities, and women develop a more assertive, aggressive approach. This means that dream images are more easily accessible

This is part of the nature/nurture debate - whether, for instance, women learn from their mothers how to be more receptive or whether they become so naturally - and this is relevant so far as dreaming is concerned. The images that come up in dreams arise initially from the store of information available to us through experience. Our perception of what goes on around us will inevitably have been coloured by our understanding. In a home where displays of affection are natural, the child (and the adult he or she becomes) will more readily express affection. Conversely, in a home where there are sexual inhibitions, the child will tend to be more apathetic. He may later discover, only when his dreams present him with images of sexual freedom, that he is by nature more outgoing than his parents. Where the stereotypes of masculine and feminine behaviour are adhered to, many people will not question the various roles until their dreams push them into considering what they feel about various issues such as sexuality.

Assuming that the baby is aware when it is born, it must have a rudimentary knowledge of what is comfortable and what is not. So, after the initial discomfort of separation from mother, the child begins to recognise its own basic need for warmth, closeness and comfort. A bonding process with mother occurs, which later on in life becomes a pattern for the child's way of relating to other people - especially the female. If his or her needs are met, then they grow with the expectation that those needs will always be met. If they are not, he or she will learn to suppress the needs. It is well known that if a young baby's demands go untended for long enough, the baby will simply stop demanding and go quiet, for it will perceive those needs as being inappropriate. If the loving, bonding process does not take place properly, then a displacement occurs which may not become recognisable until later in life, and then only in terms of the dreamer's sensuality. This may surface, for instance, as a need for close contact, or a fear of letting go. It may also arise in dreams as highly erotic images.

Example
I dreamt I was looking for something which I had lost. A beautiful

goddess-like figure dressed in black appeared and offered to help. I was very afraid of allowing her to help me, because I felt it would put me in her power.

The dreamer is probably searching for comfort. The goddess figure - which he perceives as negative - can help him to find this. He is afraid, however, to take the necessary steps which will give him what he needs.

In dreams, the adult can become aware of a whole range of feelings and emotions connected with his or her sexuality. From his early childhood and memories, there surfaces what Freud chose to call buried infantile sexuality. Freud believed that this was one of the major motivating forces behind dreaming, and saw it in terms of the penetrative act and the receptive passive act.

Bearing in mind that his society was more paternalistic (as well as being more inhibited) in its nature, it would probably be safer in today's climate to say that dreams help us to come to terms with - and to understand - our own bodily rather than sexual image. As a baby grows it becomes more and more aware of what is a pleasurable bodily experience, and what is not. As an example, if smacked for fondling mother's breast the baby may develop suppressed fears, which later may surface as a difficulty with sex. If, however, such an act is perceived as a pleasurable experience, the child will be at ease with its own body.

This is shown most clearly in a dream which most people have at some time or another. It has long been accepted that at some point we will dream of being naked. Freud believed that this was an attempt to return to a state of innocence and purity, before there was bodily awareness. In real terms such a dream may simply be an attempt for the dreamer to be more conscious of his own body. He can put to one side the burdens of everyday life and has freedom to be sensuous and sensual. Since in childhood the growth hormone is more active during sleep, it would be perfectly logical for a dreamer to be aware of the activity that is taking place in his or her own body - even if it was only subliminally - and therefore to wish to be naked. The need to be naked can therefore have more than one meaning. Firstly there is the need for freedom, secondly the need to find closeness with someone else, thirdly the need to expose one's vulnerability, and also perhaps to create a climate of honesty and openness. Being naked would only be sexually explicit if union on a physical level was taking place.

Self-image - that is, the way one perceives oneself to be - is very closely tied up with sexuality. It has been suggested that in coming to terms with the physical body, and in learning to handle the genitalia, a child very quickly recognises the pleasurable feelings associated with that part of the body, whether it is initially an act of stimulation or not. Curiosity will have the child exploring those areas of the body. As with so many other things, if that perfectly natural act is prevented or interrupted, there may be repercussions or difficulties later on. If the recognition and the taking of pleasure in bodily stimulation at this infantile level are suppressed (or indeed overly encouraged) there will be distortions and possibly deviations which can occur in adult life.

All this makes it sound as though there is only doom and gloom associated with this process of recognition. This is patently not true. We each have a right to know and to understand what can - and will - give us pleasure on a physical level. It is this early learning process which is such an intrinsic part of our sexual enjoyment later on. Sensuality is such a significant part of sexuality and self-enjoyment that if there are problems with this - perhaps in a new relationship - the mind will often trawl for information and produce images in dreams which will help us to understand ourselves better. Thus when we are exploring new ways of being close to someone we can often have dreams about our childhood or previous relationships.

In a young child at the time of increased bodily awareness the dreaded process of 'potty training' also takes place. For many people there is a great deal of confusion which still presents itself in relation to sexuality and toilet training. What is important is that, through toilet training, the child first begins to appreciate that it can have control over its own bodily functions. It can also have a modicum of power over other people around it. The situation where the child is placed on the potty and expected to perform is well known. Two minutes later, after no result, it has wet its pants with great glee. Often in later years dreams surface around the issues of control and conformity, as well as performance expectations and anxieties. These may or may not be overtly sexual or with a sexual element within them.

Example
I dreamt I was watching a chorus of girls performing in some kind of a musical review. It struck me that the whole audience were men. Each man could control one of the dancers, and all the dancers were being manipulated. I was also trying to control a dancer but not very successfully. When I realised it was my mother I was controlling, I woke up.

Self-image is also very closely tied up with the feedback we receive from other people. There is nowhere from which we will receive more honest feedback than in an intimate relationship, and often a dream which has a sexual content will perform the function of confirming our own good feelings about ourselves. Working again on the theory that what or who we dream about is also part of ourselves, we seek and achieve self-approval in the sexual dream.

RELATIONSHIPS

When the child has formed an image of itself, and how and whether the basic needs are going to be satisfied or not, it begins to learn how to relate to other people. Obviously the child's first relationships are with its parents, and those interactions form the bedrock of how he or she will relate to other members of the opposite and of the same sex. This first view will be changed and refined according to experience.

Because these relationships are so important, it is quite natural and appropriate that at the age of about four there will be some kind of an erotic charge between child, and - usually - the parent of the opposite sex. If this charge is handled sensitively the child goes on to learn and mature, learning all the time. He or she begins to accept certain behaviour as being appropriate and other as not. It is common at this time to see the little girl 'flirting' with father or father figure as she begins to recognise her own instinctive power. It is equally common to observe the little boy becoming solicitous over his mother's welfare. If the child becomes confused during this period there is the potential for such feelings to be suppressed, denied or exaggerated. These child-like responses may surface in later years as dream images of incest and eroticism. This type of dream is dealt with more fully in the chapter on deviations. For men, they must escape from female domination, to an easy sexual relationship with women, and an appreciation of their own masculinity, where they are not in competition with father. Women, however, must recognise that their first bonding in both a sexual and sensual way will have been with mother, only later to be followed by a bonding with father. A woman will often initially seek a partner who shows similar characteristics to both parents.

There is a further stage in the growth process - around puberty - when the relationship with parents or other adult members of the family surfaces with sexual overtones. As the teenager begins to move away from close involvement with the family to experiment with other relationships, the security of a known emotion can be translated into sexual feelings or 'fancying' the parent of the opposite sex. If this is recognised as a transient phase no harm is done, although teenagers can become very worried by dreams of having sex with a parent.

Dream images hold an element of past experience. It is therefore obvious that overtly sexual dreams can be more easily accepted when we have some understanding of how we grew into the person we are at this time. If we have not gained such an understanding, then the sexual act is more likely to be symbolised and perhaps less easily recognised. We may, for instance, dream of shooting someone or being shot, or of being bitten by a snake.

As we move into adulthood we can become aware of certain basic blueprints and ideals that we hold in our subconscious. The most easily recognisable ones are the knight in shining armour - which every woman will recognise - or the damsel in distress who needs rescuing. These blueprints - which Jung believed were held by everyone - can become distorted by childhood experiences, socialisation and even parental experience.

Our basic instinctual urge to reproduce in the most effective way possible begins with fantasy, moves through dreams and should culminate in successful sexual relationships. Archetypes, belonging as they do to a pool of the collective unconscious, allow us to access a huge source of information and knowledge as symbols and pictures. These enable us successfully to create a life for ourselves, where we are properly supported and nurtured. By coming to an understanding of the illusions and distortions we ourselves create - and which can be created for us by other people - we are able to adjust our waking lives for personal success. These archetypes often are produced initially in dreams, as images, and then assimilated and recognised in everyday life. We can safely dream of a sexual relationship with an ideal figure without harming ourselves or others.

While there are other archetypal figures which appear in dreams, those that are pertinent in dreams of a sexual nature are those which are associated most with the masculine and feminine attributes within our character. It is easy to understand this concept if we remember that we are conceived out of a coming together of the masculine and feminine. We will therefore have inherited certain character traits from both mother and father. They in turn will have inherited characteristics and behaviours from their parents, who will have had to make sense of their parents' idiosyncrasies. Jung became fascinated by the way that the mind creates symbols and characterisations, which appear to be common to all mankind. In tandem with his work on archetypes, it was he who first divided the functions of the mind into four aspects; sensation, feeling, thinking and intuition. Later work by his pupils confirmed the existence of both masculine and feminine archetypes. It is now possible to develop a kind of pathway through the various interactions which occur within the personality, and more often than not become reflected outwards into relationship, whether sexual or otherwise.

The first thing which needs to be understood is that regardless of our overt gender, there is an inner side of our personality that is of the opposite gender. Thus the male will have a hidden female side, and the female will have hidden masculine characteristics. This hidden side will be affected by information received throughout life. If that hidden side is denied or repressed, it will often surface in dream images as a man or a woman, sometimes recognisable by the dreamer and sometimes not. An ideal of what this internal masculine or feminine figure should be is formed very early on through one's relationships with one's parents, although this may later become distorted by external experience. This internal figure is called the Anima in the masculine, and the Animus in the feminine. As part of the growing-up process young people begin relationships outside the family. At this point it is very easy to project this ideal onto their partner. They try to make their partners conform to that ideal, rather than allowing them to be themselves.

It is probably impossible for any one human being to be able to totally satisfy the needs of another, whether those needs are emotional or sexual. Indeed it is a sign of maturity when we realise that both we and our partner are going to require different things from different people. There is then no further need to agonise over relationships where, for instance, a husband finds himself becoming jealous of his wife's relationship with her mother. Often the content of his dreams will give him the opportunity to work his feelings out in such a way that there is benefit all round.

Example
I dreamt that my wife and I were waiting for her parents in a bar. They came in, and my wife immediately crossed over and sat on her mother's knee (something she would not do in real life). I found this very erotic, but I didn't know who I fancied, my wife or her mother. I think her mother is an old battle-axe in real life.

In this dream, there is an instinctive recognition that his wife is still maintaining the mother/daughter relationship, which he now finds attractive rather than threatening. It is mother-in-law's personality that he is ambivalent over.

The feminine qualities in a man at best help him to understand his more caring and sensitive side. At worst they become destructive, and put him in a position of acting in an unstable fashion. For instance, he may find himself unable to decide between two courses of action, or between two women. In dreams this can manifest as a dream where his partner changes into the other woman, or vice versa. When he recognises that he can correct that instability within himself, he is able to accept that the dream figures can help him to understand himself.

Instead of being a figure to be feared, this internal feminine can be developed as a friend and ally. Recognised properly, the Anima becomes the Muse of the poet, the Inspirer of the musician, the Motivator of the businessman. When he appreciates that there is a potential for an inner union to take place, his dreams will often take on a sexual quality which signifies this union. He is thus able to access a vast amount of awareness and knowledge which has hitherto been unavailable to him. He will then find himself more able to be successful in relationships in everyday life, whether sexual or otherwise.

In dreams the Anima can appear in numerous forms, sometimes showing herself as an unknown woman, as a goddess figure, as someone known to the dreamer, and often as an aspect of his own mother. This is because a man internalises his own perception of the feminine around him because of his early relationship with his mother. The latter will have formed the lodestone of his relationship with women. It is often not until he meets someone who has come to terms with herself as woman, that he will be able to release the perceptions and energy he has kept pent up.

These first releases and experimentation will often manifest as sexual dreams. For instance, in an attempt to discover his mother's sexuality he may dream of watching her - or perhaps a dream character who represents her - acting, in his view, in an inappropriate manner sexually. He may dream of her behaving with considerable abandonment, when in actual fact she is somewhat self-contained in real life. Conversely she may in dreams appear to be inhibited when she is a very open person. It is almost as though he is testing out his hypotheses about women in his dream scenarios.

Particularly if his mother has inhibited his sexual growth in some way, he will have difficulty in reconciling his own needs with those of the women around him. He will often expect to be mothered by his partner and become very confused when this does not happen. When he realises however that women have the ability to be 'other than mother' he will be able to deal with that expectation, and to move into a full relationship with his partner. He will allow his partner to express all the feminine archetypes as appropriate, and will not try to inhibit her self-expression. Many men at this present time are struggling with the fact that women no longer perceive themselves simply as nurturers and carers, but want equality in all areas. This struggle will often give rise to dreams which have a sexual content. Sometimes that content will demonstrate his need to dominate the feminine, almost as though he expects to control her through the use of his own sexuality. At other times he will be aware that he is being dominated by the woman, which may give rise to dreams of sadism. This aspect is dealt with more fully in the chapter on deviations.

If a man does not fully come to terms with the realisation that no real woman can actually be his ideal woman, there is a danger that he will project onto some fantasy figure all his longings and desires. Thus his fantasies may appear more 'real' than a proper fulfilling relationship with a woman, and he is left unable to communicate properly, because the fantasy gets in the way of reality. Often dreams will attempt to balance out this unhealthy attitude, so that he can create proper relationships.

Example
I've just started seeing a new lady. From the time I was a teenager I've had a very clear view as to what my partner would be like. I had a dream whereby this person was fighting with my new friend. I was very sad because in the dream I realised I was going to have to choose which one to be with, and I didn't want to have to do that.

If a man presents an exceptionally macho image to the world it is often because he is fearful of the feminine, more spontaneous side of his personality. Equally if he is of a more gentle nature, the more assertive side of him will show itself in dreams as a more sexually active dream character until he has learnt to achieve a proper balance between the two.

If a man has too much of a negative concept of the feminine, rather than fantasising about an ideal, he will in real life project onto his partner or other women around him all the faults he sees in that concept. There comes a time when for his own integration he must relinquish those projections. Dreams will often help him to do this.

Example
My wife and I have not been getting on well. She is very shy, a bit like my sister, and when we first married I could accept that. My job now means I need a partner who can keep up with me. I had a dream where my sister and I were very young, and she was refusing to come to school because she was ill. I promised that I would bring her school books home.

The inner feminine becomes the guide to inner wisdom only when a man confronts his destructive side and learns how to handle the energy he has available. Often he will protect himself from understanding himself by working and playing in an exclusively male environment, and it is only when he persistently has dreams which have a sexual content that he is alerted to his own fears and doubts.

Just as a man has a hidden feminine side, so the woman has a hidden masculine. This part, when properly understood, enables her to develop the logical deliberating side of herself, and to develop self-awareness. Her masculine side and her perception of the masculine will have been affected by her early contact with the men around her. It is interesting to note that, if they have not developed their own understanding of themselves, the woman's inner masculine will reflect this. She may find that she uses a distorted judgement founded on wrong perceptions that she has never felt the need to question, and it is only when dreams force her to look at those perceptions that she is able to develop her own judgement properly.

Example
I dreamt I was a judge in a rape trial. (I had just been badly let down by my boyfriend, though not raped.) My father suddenly appeared in the dream, and said 'Well, she must have deserved it.' It made me realise how much I had allowed myself to become a casualty.

Often, if the woman has over-developed the negative side of the Animus she will feel that she has to compete with men, or to be destructive to other women. Dreams, and particularly sexual ones, will often try to redress this balance and make her aware of the difficulties that this can give her.

Example

I dreamt I had applied for a job in a brothel. I was perfectly confident in my dream, until I realised all the other applicants were men.

Usually the masculine shows itself in dreams to alert the woman to the fact that she needs to develop - or conversely, has overdeveloped - the more logical strategic side of her personality. If she is unable to recognise this, she will often project her difficulties onto her partner and have unreal expectations of him. She may feel he is unable to look after her properly, that he has no ambition, that he cannot cope with the demands made on him and so on. Often dreams with a sexual content to them will show the way to redressing the balance.

Example

In my dream I was headmistress in a school for prostitutes. For some reason I insisted that the girls called me 'Sir'. Then my husband came in and I handed my cane to him. (Since the cane is a symbol of masculine sexuality, the dreamer is in fact giving her husband back his masculinity.)

Particularly in this day and age, women's perceptions of themselves are changing. The drive towards the more assertive feminine has been echoed in the enhanced opportunities for women and in the changes in fashion. When a woman is prepared to acknowledge the more masculine side of her personality much benefit can be gained, but there does need to be a balance established. This often can become apparent in dreams, particularly those of a sexual character.

The following dream is more fully interpreted in the dream interpretation section.

Example
I was walking on a beach, at first alone, and then met a man I didn't know. We had to build a sand castle, and then I knew we would have sex. When I looked at the sand castle it was in the shape of a computer.

Sexual dreams allow us to access all of the characteristics which make each of us unique. When we have understood both the masculine and feminine sides of our personality, we can allow ourselves to manage them in waking life and to take advantage of the energy released. There may be at times conflict between the masculine attributes and the feminine ones, but once some kind of a balance is established the richness of the whole self can lead to a much greater awareness, and a greatly enhanced lifestyle.

MADONNA vs. WHORE AND HERO vs. VILLAIN

By dividing women into the archetypes of good and bad women, madonnas and whores, nice girls and sluts, men try to diminish the influence that women have - and have had - over them since the moment of birth. They, in this way, attempt to avoid the confusion of both their own - and women's - sexuality by pushing women into either of those roles without paying attention to any other aspects of woman's personality. This can cause difficulties all round, which the dreamer may not resolve until he recognises through dreams his dependency on one type or the other. When the whore or frankly seductive woman appears in his dreams and fantasies, it is time to explore his attitude to his own beliefs and the way in which he treats his women. When he consistently dreams of mother or fantasises about a mother figure, he is trying to compartmentalise women so that he feels he has an element of control over them. However, when a man actually dreams of having sex with such a figure, he must dig deeper into his own psyche and recognise that she will not devour him. He can combine the best qualities of woman into someone to whom he can relate without fear. This knowledge can itself be scary, and often initially can only be accepted by dreaming about it.

Example
I was with my mother at the seaside. (We went regularly to the seaside when I was a child.) I was afraid she wouldn't let me go out for the day with the woman down the road. I told her I was old enough to know what I was doing.

Mothers are most often men's first experience of women. Because needs frequently remain unresolved, most people continue to be enmeshed in that primary relationship. The biggest myth about masculinity is that men are independent and free of emotional needs. Freud wrote that men can't make a clear transition from their love of their mothers to a sexual love for women. He said that men tend to debase women to whom they are sexually attracted and to over-evaluate women they love. Mothers and wives are supposedly idealised, but women whom men perceive as sexual objects are abused. The sexual harassment of girls at school is evidence of this. Teenage boys seem to possess a spiteful need to denounce girls as sluts and slags as they shape their independence from their mothers.

The Victorian years were a prime example of this twofold standard, dividing women into archetypes of mothers and whores. Within the home, father cosseted and adored (or completely ignored) the feminine mystery of his wife. She was either an adornment to his household, or a drudge to be used in whatever way he saw fit. The prostitute, however, was there when his appetites became too gross for this paragon to cope with, or when she was pregnant or had just had a child.

Nowadays the balance of power, if it can be called this, is shifting. Men have always liked sexuality 'hard' while women have preferred it 'soft'. While men will readily view pornography, women need erotic stimulation. Women want the whole person, but men home in on specific parts of the body. Men tend to be stimulated by vital parts, while women are stimulated by relationships. Men lust, women yearn. Dreams about sex will often contain elements of the opposite - or even the more suppressed - aspect of the self. Men will dream about their own more sensitive side, while women will dream of the more assertive.

The idea that pornography leads inevitably to rape is patently somewhat ludicrous. The viewing of fantasy women with perfect physical attributes is an obvious trigger for masculine arousal. The blatantly sexual images portrayed in pornography can often crystallise a man's image of what he wants in a sexual partner. These images can then appear in dreams almost as though he were holding a dress rehearsal. Such dreams will allow him to face his fears and doubts, before attempting a 'proper' relationship with a real woman.

Women's need for erotica is less for a sexual image and more an image of beauty. Women are much more likely to be 'turned on' by a well-formed masculine body, rather than lewd sexual poses. Equally, the image which her eventual partner will portray is likely to be less important than the qualities he possesses. Erotic dream images may enable her to be selective within the process of moving towards a fulfilling partnership. As ideas become more liberated, the squeaky-clean 'boy next door' image gives way to the 'body builder' type, first recognised as attractive within the gay world. Women do tend to appreciate that this is often unattainable in everyday life.

Example
I dreamt I was at a male stripper show. The men were all very beautiful, tall, clean-cut American types. They formed a pyramid with their bodies on one side of the stage. Then my boyfriend, who is quite short, came on stage, and jumped to the top of the pyramid. He fitted in very well, but I realised I didn't want him to be there.

Feminine fantasies start with the idea that they need to be taken away from whatever circumstances they find themselves in. The mythological idea that they need to be rescued from the dragon by the knight in shining armour is probably a representation of the killing off of their own passionate nature, in favour of devotion to their chosen mate. Reality, however, tends not to support this; many women are left with the fantasy and also the dream that they - at some point in their lives - will be swept off their feet. Many of a woman's dreams, until she begins to recognise her own power, will contain such images. Her 'knight' in today's world, however, is more likely to be a work colleague, or some other powerful male. She will often stop short of sexual intercourse, since she is more likely to fantasise about what it might be like, rather than face the actuality of the deed. An extension of this dream is when the woman dreams of her own ability to have her knight remove his armour and to be seduced by her.

Many fantasies and dreams which women have will centre around the unattainable. These may range from sex with her father, to sex or a passionate relationship with famous figures such as pop stars, or even characters from fiction. Often these characters will have an element of the villain about them which can only be tamed by the woman herself. This echoes the dichotomy which men experience between the madonna and the whore, although in a woman's case it is between the prince and the villain. It is only when she realises that she has a right to assert herself within a sexual relationship and to ensure that her own needs can be met, that she is able to use her own power constructively.

Example

I have a fairly high-powered job - which I enjoy - as personal assistant to a managing director. In my dream I had to go away on business with my boss, who I do not fancy at all. My husband wanted me to stay at home and accused me of having an affair with my boss. I told him that was ridiculous, as it was he with whom I wanted to have a baby (thus revealing her own hidden desire). In reality we have consciously decided not to have children yet.

For a man sexual maturity means that he has come to terms with the apparent 'internal split' between mother figure (madonna) and sexual being (whore). A woman must understand the difference between a romantic idealisation of the masculine (hero) and the self-seeking male (villain) in order to become sexually mature. Thus, as they become individuals in their own right, they are able to differentiate between what they consider to be an ideal relationship and one that will work in everyday life.

TEENAGE DREAMS

During the teenage years, and particularly round about the age of fourteen to sixteen, there are two different needs which arise. One is to understand oneself, and the other is to make sense of the world one lives in. As consistent threads running through this time are the hormonal changes which go on in order to prepare the child for 'the act of procreation'. The bodily changes which take place can be confusing enough without taking into account the mental changes, the need for independence and yet the searching for an intimate relationship. This usually is with the opposite sex, and will eventually satisfy the needs of which the teenager is only just becoming aware. All this requires the breaking away from previously held ideas and possibly family beliefs, and the development of a belief system which works at a very deep level for the young person alone.

The time of puberty is therefore a time when a great deal of information needs sorting and understanding, and much of this can be accomplished in the dream state. Initially the images are those which can be easily interpreted, such as trying to escape, fighting with something or perhaps climbing a tree or a mountain - something which represents an obstacle to progress. The dreaming mind will then present images of opposites, to be compared and contrasted, big/small, good/bad, open/closed, masculine/feminine etc. The teenager may not at this stage be prepared to accept overtly sexual images, so symbols of masculinity, (for instance, pointed objects) and of femininity (round bags or containers) may appear. Then images of people and of intimacy or of intimate situations will appear which will often be comforting and very intense. This process of dreaming obviously does not necessarily take place in order, and can often appear in the same dream.

Example
I dreamt I was running down a hill, trying to escape from a huge monster. My boyfriend appeared, and threw something at it, which I realised was a sports javelin from school. Next thing I was in bed with him, and then my brother came in and sat on the end of the bed.

Running down the hill suggests the need to escape from a feeling or emotion which is too big to handle (the monster). The boyfriend then is able to protect her by using his masculinity (the javelin). School is also considered to be a safe space. The dreamer is at ease with her boyfriend, although perhaps less sexually involved than is at first apparent, since her brother then appears on the scene.

It is quite common for young people at this time to be very disturbed by dreaming of a parent's death. This is in fact a perfectly acceptable dream in the maturing process. By 'dying', the parent no longer has authority over the youngster, and he or she must take responsibility for his or her own life. The death leaves the field clear for other relationships. Actively killing the parent in dreams, while shocking, also suggests the recognition of the teenager's ability to leave the family environment and be free to explore a wider world. This obviously does not mean that the parent is going to die or be killed in real life.

This type of dream is a playing out of the conflict which occurs in the animal kingdom when the leader of the pack is challenged. If this right to leave the parents of one's own freewill is not possible, either because the parent has left, been taken away, or because circumstances have not permitted the child to make the break themselves, there may be difficulty in relating successfully with other people in a sexually fulfilling way. Only later, perhaps when this type of dream surfaces in adult life, can the dilemma be resolved.

For a young man the conflict with father in dreams is often the first awareness of his emerging manhood. Following this he will often dream of a mysterious feminine figure, which is totally unattainable and with whom the relationship is certainly not sexual. This usually symbolises his breaking away from his mother, and his perception of taboos which will operate at this time. It is also the emergence of the inner feminine or Anima - who may or may not become a guiding principle.

It is also at this time that the young man is likely to have conflict between the need to be mothered and sexual experience (See Madonna vs Whore chapter). Dreams are likely to become much more sexually orientated and to actually depict sexual intimacy. This type of dream often does not, however, occur until the youngster has dared to explore his sexuality on the physical level. When he realises that he neither needs to have power over a woman, nor to be afraid of his own emerging sexuality, he can mature into a successful individual.

Example

I am a sixteen-year-old boy. I dreamt my family and I were emigrating to Australia. On the ship I met a girl I fancied. We were sitting talking when my father came in. I was very afraid the girl would find him more attractive than I. I then realised she looked like my mother and it didn't matter anyway.

For a young woman the conflicts are slightly different. She must first come to terms with her relationships with her mother and then with her father. Her connection with her mother was initially one of physical intimacy, whereas her relationship with her father tends to be slightly more distant. She must therefore recognise that she must change her ability to relate to her father. Often this depicts itself as dreams of sexual intimacy with her father which can be very frightening. Her first real relationships with other men are likely to be either totally unsuitable or with older father figures. Dreams at this time can point her in the direction in which she is capable of developing.

Example

I am fifteen. I dreamt I was a child playing on the beach with my father. He suddenly picked me up and started throwing me up in the air. My present boyfriend (who my parents do not like) was standing in the background. I asked my father to put me down, which he did. I then realised there was another man standing behind my boyfriend, and I 'knew' this was the person I would leave with.

This dream depicts the emergence of the Animus or inner masculine as a helpful figure and is also interpreted more fully in the Dreams chapter.

Throughout the transition from puberty to adulthood, a girl is growing into the unique person she will become. She will become aware of the need for intimacy, the desire to attract and the ability to have a baby. Dreams are often a safe space in which to 'practise' these activities. Initially the teenager may feel herself to be trapped or being made to do something she does not wish to do. Her dreams may indicate whether she is trapped by limitations imposed on her by her family or by her own developing beliefs about herself.

Many teenage girls' dreams come into the category of 'reassurance dreams'. A teenage girl will usually need to know first that she is loveable, secondly that she is a capable human being and lastly that she is able to create something of her own which she can love. It is perhaps unfortunate that, because boys of her own age will be going through their own developmental changes, she is not able to obtain that reassurance from them and almost inevitably in waking life will seek that reassurance from a more mature individual.

Through dreams she may be able to decide for herself what actions she should take in order to fulfil her own needs. She may, for instance, dream of an intimate situation with a teacher or some other unattainable figure, only to realise later that this person symbolises the type of partnership she is looking for. She is not in love with this person, she is simply attracted to him.

As she grows and matures - particularly if she is helped sensitively - she will become aware of her own sense of specialness, and ultimately of her own power. Many of her dreams will carry within them some aspect of having a secret, which must not be revealed to others. This is the essential intuitive power of woman, which frightens most men, but is the right of every woman. When she is at ease with her own sexuality and with her own inner connection she becomes a very powerful person in her own right.

In an ideal world, young people having worked out what they want, and having matured into well-rounded wonderful adults, will form relationships with people who most closely approximate their dream partner and will live happily ever after. Unfortunately this does not often happen. Throughout childhood the young person will have internalised many of their parents' attitudes, beliefs and fears. When they reach the teenage years, as well as trying to come to terms with their own emerging sexuality, they also must question and understand their parents' sexuality. This can be quite a disturbing time as they find out that their parents are capable of deep feelings, that they may not feel about sex in the same way as their parents, and even that the secure family unit is not so secure after all. In today's climate (where one in three marriages ends in divorce) the teenager may find that he or she is having to cope with multiple relationships. Both mother and father may remarry, which may mean the young person has to cope with forming non-sexual relationships with both new partners, their children and any babies born of the new relationships. Dreams can be a way of releasing the tensions which may be generated in such situations, particularly the sexual ones.

Example
I dreamt my half-sister and I were at the swimming pool. I am sixteen, she is fifteen. I was watching her dive. I suddenly realised that I fancied her. Does this mean I'm weird?

The answer of course is no, but there are certain restrictions imposed by society which this boy would be sensible to follow. He is aware that he is capable of being aroused, but it is not appropriate for him to change the relationship with his half-sister. He is able to make choices.

A young person's own choice of partner at this time may not be very good either. Until they have made a few mistakes they may not be able to decide what their particular style of approach needs to be. This can be a time when dreams allow them to experiment both with different partners and with different approaches to the opposite sex. They themselves are not hurt by these dream excursions, and neither is anyone else. Other dreams can also help the young people to decide how they would wish to be approached.

Dreams at this stage can also alert them to the fact that there is more than one way of being intimate with other people.

Finally the young person may find that, through a series of dreams, he or she can grow in understanding of sexuality and can come to terms with their own self-image, their need for relationship and support by the opposite sex, progressing on to a mature and loving relationship with the rest of the world.

HOMOSEXUALITY

There are numerous theories as to why homosexuality arises, which are not being dealt with here except in the context of dreams. In working with dreams, it is vital to understand that it is the internal balance between the masculine and feminine sides of the personality which gives rise to dreams with a homosexual element. It is more than probable that there is less evidence of this type of dream because the majority of people are too ashamed to record them, lest they be thought 'queer'. Once reassured that such dreams are part of a perfectly normal process, and can be seen as an attempt to integrate the two sides of the personality, they become more acceptable and understandable.

While we may be overtly heterosexual, there is also a part of us that at some point has at least been curious about relationships with the same sex. There are two ways in which dreams of, or about, homosexuality need to be considered. The first is easily recognised because within each individual there is a unique blend of aspects of the masculine and feminine. Some of these aspects are more overt than others. The way in which we develop in response to our own needs and to family and social pressure - backed up by inherited characteristics - helps determine which of these aspects we will use more often. As a way of trying to create balance between the logical and intuitional sides of our personalities, parts which have been suppressed or not understood can surface in dreams about homosexuality and lesbianism.

Creativity and sexuality are very closely bound together. As an expression of creativity the sexual act is well recognised and, as mentioned elsewhere in this book, our prime need in a partner is someone who is similar to ourselves in as many ways as possible. We need to rely on that person to supply love and support in a way that is right for us. In waking life, those whose search for sexual partnership is more overt are labelled promiscuous, and those whose search includes members of the same sex as themselves are labelled homosexual or lesbian. (While the word homosexual is generally taken as coming from the Latin word for man, it in fact comes from the Greek word for same, as in homogeneous.) It is this group of people whose dreams also need to be considered and understood in the light of their own lifestyle.

In early childhood the sensual needs to be held and comforted are important. The child at that time becomes very aware of its own sensitivity. Then during the teenage years there is often confusion over sexual needs. This is triggered off partly by hormonal changes, but also by changes of perception. The natural sensitivity that a child has towards others changes into a more self-centred attitude and can give rise to huge self-doubts. As mentioned elsewhere, if these doubts are not handled properly the child can perceive himself or herself as needing more from one parent (often the parent of the same sex as themselves) than the other. When the child is uncomfortable with the feedback he receives, (such as not being understood, having to do things which go against his own nature, etc.) a boy may, in response, develop a degree of overt femininity. Girls may develop the masculine side of themselves, possibly in an attempt to please father or - conversely - to hide their developing femininity.

This confusion may be hidden, only to surface later on in dreams in various ways as part of the growing process. The need to see oneself as a powerful human being may be perceived as a compulsion for intercourse or union with someone of the same gender. This then may emphasise the earlier need for physical closeness. In dreams this can surface as actual intercourse, as a means of stressing the intensity of the desire for physical touch.

If, in a boy's case, there has perhaps been a weak or absent father, his connection with his mother may be particularly strong. This may mean that his perceptions of his world are slightly biased towards a more sensitive perception. Every girl's first relationship is with her mother, and the initial need is for sensitivity and nurturing.

Example
The night before this dream I had had an awful argument with my

father. I am a sixteen-year old boy. I dreamt that I was at a huge party and was physically attracted to an older man. I realised in the dream that this man was a very weak character, and not at all the sort of person I really liked.

The fears, doubts and questions which arise in dreams for most people in relation to their perception of themselves as being different or more sensitive can often be expressed through dreams which have a strong erotic content. It is almost as though the sense of not belonging or of perceiving things differently from other people can be handled through such dreams. The intensity of feeling, passion and anxiety has to be suppressed in everyday life, but is totally permissible in dreams. The internal struggle between the need to be dominant and the need to submit within relationships often translates itself into the dream scenario through dreams of sex with members of the same gender as oneself. Such dreams allow the individual to understand and come to terms with a perceived lack of masculinity or femininity within themselves in a safe and appropriate way. This then allows them to accept their own make-up more easily, and, with that understanding, to relate to others of a similar nature.

Fear of long-term relationships and the need to prove one's sexual competency often lead to promiscuity and infidelity. Particularly within the gay world, this is recognised and, while not necessarily always liked, the need for multiple partners is accepted. Sexual activity as an expression of immediate mutual attraction is accepted as normal, as is sex for comfort and friendship. These standards are less easily accepted within the heterosexual environment, and therefore can sometimes only be expressed in dreams of homosexuality.

When the individual deliberately rejects the norm within the society within which he or she exists, there is a tremendous loneliness. The person recognises that they are in the minority, and the search for partnership is widened into the search for a group of like-minded people. That group of people is likely to have its own customs, beliefs and structures. Over a period of time these will be internalised by the new entrant, and will become part of their way of thought. Within the gay communities (both lesbian and homosexual) there is the expectation of openness and acceptance in matters to do with sexuality and relationship not often seen within the heterosexual world. There is also a recognition of eroticism in its truest sense - the arousal of sexual passion and excitement - and the appreciation of beauty in all its forms. Thus, eroticism in dreams is more easily accepted, as is the personal expression of that eroticism. Fewer inhibiting factors applied at a conscious level mean that erotic dreams and dreams with a sexual content are more easily accepted, and perhaps more easily understood within the context of the dreamer's lifestyle.

The following dream, which was part of a larger one, is more fully interpreted in the Dreams section.

Example
I was with my partner. We were in a settlement - not a town, but not a village either. We went up a very steep hill which looked like a forest. On the hill there were 'discarded' railway carriages. Some of them had been turned into homes 'illegally'. I felt they were being squatted rather than being properly inhabited. Some of the carriages were rusty and had not been put to any use and I went inside a couple of them. I was hoping for a sexual encounter inside the dark carriages. It was as though actually entering the carriages had a strongly sexual connotation. No sexual encounter took place.

The settlement here suggests the gay lifestyle, since it is neither a conventional town or village, but more a way of life. The illegal homes, which are not being used for their proper purpose, suggest something outside the law, and stand for temporary resting places (perhaps one-night stands). Looking for a sexual encounter is seen as a perfectly normal activity given the dreamer's lifestyle, and the fact that the carriages are darkened suggests that he does not wish to take responsibility for what happens. The erotic charge is in actually looking for sex.

Homo-eroticism (physical arousal by a member of the same sex) and homophobia (hatred and fear of homo-eroticism) are at opposite ends of a sexual spectrum. In dreams, to be aroused by a member of the same sex alerts us to our sexual appreciation of others. It also highlights our masculinity or femininity. Homophobia in dreams, as in waking life, touches in on a deeply held fear of being abnormal. This fear, without understanding oneself, can erupt in everyday life into persecution and oppression of others. A homophobic reaction is a defence mechanism against lack of knowledge. Dreams can assist people, especially men, to learn more about - and to understand - themselves. Many people dislike the idea of being sensitive, only to discover that many of these sensitivities are suppressed within themselves.

Finally, in understanding homosexuality and lesbianism it is perhaps necessary to acknowledge the spiritual component in such self-expression. It is every person's right to search for union with his or her own spirituality - that inner peace and tranquillity - which many people find through organised religion and ritual. While most such religions abhor what they call 'abnormal sexual practices' none would deny the right to that search. Each person must carry out that search in his or her own unique way, which also means understanding oneself and one's fellow man. That spiritual union can, in fact, only take place on an inner level, to allow an outward expression of the creativity innate in each one of us. Dreams are a creative expression of that union.

DEVIATIONS

It is important to realise that although many dreams can have in them elements of what seem to be deviations from normal sexual practices, this does not mean that the dreamer is sexually perverted. This material is simply the mind's way of presenting a process that is going on (or perhaps needs to go on) at an internal, mostly unconscious, level to ensure the dreamer's health. Fantasies that have an element of perversion in them should be thought of as a more conscious process that may have some danger in it for the dreamer, since it is a more directed activity.

Bestiality

Very occasionally dreams occur which contain practices that are totally alien to the dreamer. Bestiality or the desire for sex with an animal can be totally inexplicable, unless one understands that this is simply the mind's way of translating and presenting in graphic terms an aggressive impulse that could be harmful. The dreaming mind will remove the taboos imposed on the conscious self in order to have the individual recognise how powerful his lower more instinctive urges are. Pagan belief suggested that such now unnatural practices could give one greater power.

Fetishism

Dreaming of fetishism is slightly different from the practice of fetishism in real life. By fastening on a particular object as part of a sexual 'ritual' in dreams, the mind is enabled to concentrate on the object as much as the sexual act. Thus it is the symbolism of the object that is relevant. The information is that we cannot do without this 'thing' in our lives, and must do everything we can to provide ourselves with it. For instance, dreaming of a fetish over women's clothing would suggest a need to develop the more feminine sexually sensitive part. Dreaming of a cuddly toy might suggest the need for more tenderness. A fetish in a dream might indicate the need for more control during the sexual act. The use of a fetish suggests a kind of displacement mechanism - a way of directing the mind away from the actual activity.

It is this last technique that is most used in fantasy, whether the individual fastens on a particular object as part of the fantasy, or, as some people do, uses fantasy itself as a fetish. This suggests not being able carry out the sexual act without fantasising at the same time.

Incest

Dreaming of sexual activity with - usually - the opposite sex parent is a natural part of maturing. As stated elsewhere, the teenager particularly may go through a process of being erotically attracted to that parent, only to realise that that attraction is inappropriate and should be directed outward beyond the family. When the dreams are of sex with - or a sexual attraction to - other members of the family, the dream self is creating a particular scenario. This is where the conscious mind can come to terms with the taboos which are present in society. The individual has to learn to accept or reject those taboos, and can then learn to control and use the power that it has. On a slightly more esoteric level, the dreamer may recognise the fact that he or she needs to assimilate many of the qualities belonging to the other person in the dream.

Example

I dreamt I was in bed with my uncle. We were going to have sex, but I was very frightened in the dream, and wanted my mother. I am very fond of my uncle, and am very proud of him in waking life, but I've never thought of him sexually. I'd be surprised if he thought of me in this way.

This dream indicates that the girl is growing up, and is almost ready to take control of her own sexuality. She still feels she needs the comfort of an authority figure (her mother), who can differentiate between right and wrong.

Incestuous dreams can also highlight other types of abuse, which may not necessarily be sexual. Sometimes inadvertently other members of our family can hurt us by not loving us in the way we need to be loved. They can penetrate our personal space in a way that may be hurtful to us. When we are ready to deal with that type of hurt, dreams of incest may surface. It cannot be stressed too strongly that such dreams do not necessarily mean that the individual was in fact abused. It is the perception of the individual that is relevant (When working with dream interpretation, care should be taken not to develop 'false memory syndrome' - a condition where a 'memory' is accepted as a fact, when it is simply a perception of an event).

Incest in dreams can also alert us to situations that occur in our waking life. For instance, if our partner has similar qualities to one or both of our parents, dreams of incest may occur to alert us to certain patterns of behaviour either in ourselves or our partner. We may perhaps have a tendency to be a victim within certain situations, and need to handle these more positively.

Example

I dreamt I was in bed with my lover. We were having very passionate and erotic sex. I climaxed in the dream and then realised my lover had turned into my father. In my dream I felt very cheated.

Masochism

Just as sadism is the need to hurt someone else, so masochism is the ability to accept hurt from another person. This highlights the dreamer's ability to become a victim. Once again this need not necessarily be only in a sexual sense. Many people are aroused by rough treatment, and such a dream may suggest the need for some kind of balance. Sado-masochism, where both sadism and masochism are inter-linked, is a perversion of the ordinary give-and-take which occurs in relationships. To have such a dream can alert us to extreme behaviour in either ourselves or others.

In fantasy, we give ourselves permission to do things we would not normally dare to do; for instance, allowing ourselves to be bound and held down during sex would fulfil our need for masochism.

Paedophilia

There are dreams that occur where there is a strong concentration on some kind of union with a child. Sometimes this can be simply a yearning for a particular child, or can be a desire for closeness, which in waking life is inappropriate. This is in reality the need to come to terms with, and to understand, the child within ourselves. Often in the process of growing up we lose touch with a part of ourselves, through difficulty and trauma. Through dreams it is possible to reconnect with that part of ourselves.

The dreamer had lost her father when she was seven years old, and was now in therapy.

Example

I dreamt I was cuddling a little boy of about seven. He kept asking if I would take him to bed, but I knew if I did I would have to get into bed with him. I was not sure what to do.

This is the dreamer's way of making a connection with the part of herself that was damaged by her father's death. It was her perception of the masculine side of herself which was harmed, not the feminine.

Fantasy containing elements of paedophilia can become extremely dangerous if not controlled.

Rape

To **dream of being raped** suggests that one's personal space has been penetrated in an inappropriate way. For **a man to dream of raping a woman** would suggest that he is questioning his ability to be sensitive. While in law it is difficult to prove rape, any sexual activity which goes beyond the bounds of normality may be translated in dreams into sexual violation. Technically, it is not possible for a woman to rape a man. However, in dreams a man can feel just as violated as a woman. Conversely, a woman can become aware of her need to treat a man roughly through dreams of raping him.

There are numerous fantasies that can be built up around the need to be treated roughly which border on an act of rape.

Ritualism

A ritual is defined as a prescribed order for a ceremony or service. In sexual terms this would suggest that the sex act is performed supported by various other acts without which the individual does not achieve satisfaction. (Also see **Fetish**.) These supporting rituals do not need to be sexual in themselves although they may have sexual symbolism. For instance, **the lighting of a candle** would hold both religious and sexual significance. The flame represents the life force, while the candle is phallic. Using scented oils as part of the sexual act in order to heighten the sensual enjoyment may also be a personal ritual. Often these rituals appear in dreams to alert the dreamer to certain inner desires and requirements. Most rituals are not harmful, unless they appear as acts of sadism or masochism.

Role-playing

Role-playing occurs both in fantasy and in dreams. The most commonly recognised roles are those associated with female domination. In dreams these images usually arise in order to make the dreamer aware of his true inner feelings. In fantasy the images are used to create a sense of power within the fantasiser. This can obviously work both ways, since there can be both domination over and submission. If the dreamer is playing a particular sexual role in a dream, then this is often a way of highlighting an individual aspect of the character.

Sacrificial Acts

In sexual dreams sacrificial acts - such as blood-letting, placing a partner upon an altar, symbolic bondage and so on - usually signify the need to make some kind of dedication. This can be either dedication to the person, or turning the sexual act itself into an act of worship. This suggests that the dreamer is aware of a need for a heightened state of consciousness in order to fulfil the sexual act. It represents the coming together of the sacred and the profane.

Example

In my dream I was attending some weird ceremony. The priest performed a ritual with a lighted torch over several women who were tied to a kind of altar. I was both repelled and intrigued by what was going on.

In this dream there are the symbols of both ritual and sacrificial act. The priest represents the controlling masculine; the torch, masculinity; and the women signify the submission of the feminine. The dreamer's feelings are ambivalent about the whole scenario, indicating possibly his or her own doubts and fears about his or her own sexuality.

Sadism

When the aggressive tendencies in an individual are curbed for whatever reason, there can arise dreams of sadism at a later stage. It could be, for instance, that anger or cruelty was not seen as appropriate when the dreamer was a child, causing the individual to suppress some very natural feelings. Later this can manifest in dreams as the opposite side of the individual's self-expression. Thus a meek and mild individual may have sadistic dreams of what he or she would do to another human being were the inhibitions removed. Sadism in dreams can take many forms ranging from childlike physical cruelty such as poking at a person to a representation of domination using tools such as handcuffs, whips and so on. Bondage is an act of sadism which is often brought through into waking life. It could be said that sadism arises from a need to control - both someone else and one's surroundings.

Example

I dreamt I was in an attic which contained many instruments of torture. I knew all of these were available for me to use and found this sexually arousing. There was a very pretty girl lying on a bed. I could not decide which instrument was appropriate.

This dream is interesting in that it contains elements of sadism coupled with sexual arousal, and yet there is still some indecision as to appropriate action. The inhibitions which are applicable in everyday life still seem to apply.

Voyeurism

In dreams, we are often watching either ourselves or others. When a dream has sexual connotations, it usually suggests that we are somewhat removed from our own sexuality. Sometimes voyeurism can be represented in dreams by watching ourselves in a mirror. In this case there may be some connection with eroticism or pornography. Perhaps the dreamer has difficulty in waking life in giving him or herself over completely to enjoyment of both their partner and the physical act.

Example

I had this dream where I was watching my lover and someone else making love. I watched them climax, and then realised the other person was me. I found thinking about this very arousing.

This dream is interesting, since it then gave rise to an element of fantasy as well, in consideration of the dream.

It can be seen that there are distinct differences between these deviations in waking life and actually dreaming about them. Dreams always use deviation as an extreme means of emphasising a message. Fantasy allows the individual to play with the ideas associated with deviation without expressly carrying out the act.

FANTASIES

Sexual fantasies are very similar to dreams and use many of the same themes. The activity is more consciously directed however, and is usually well within the control of the individual. There is enough evidence around to verify that fantasy can be therapeutic, and some people feel that it is an activity that can - and perhaps should - be taught. Fantasising may or may not be accompanied by sexual activity such as masturbation, and it does seem that there are several types of fantasy.

The most obvious is perhaps one where the individual fantasises about sexual intercourse or intimacy of some kind with a person who is unattainable. This may be some favourite pop star for instance or the wife's best friend. The huge following built up around Rudolf Valentino in the 1920's was of this nature, as are the 'groupies' of nowadays. Many young people will use such fantasies quite frequently in the transition stage between puberty and adulthood.

Example
I have this fantasy that I have developed, and I can use it in any way I like. In the fantasy I am the girlfriend of the lead singer in a famous rock band. The fantasy starts at home where we are very private. Sometimes we have had sex, sometimes not. We are getting ready to go out, and I am getting dressed. Usually these clothes are quite luxuriant and expensive - not the sort of thing I would usually wear. We go to the venue, and I have to help him prepare to go on stage. I do this by giving him a massage. I get quite aroused at this point, and sometimes so does he. I don't watch him perform in the fantasy because he doesn't want me to, though in real life I would not miss a performance. When he comes off stage we go home, and get very intimate. If this happened in real life I'd be terrified, but I enjoy my fantasy.

The interesting thing about this fantasy is the fact that the themes are very clear. They are those of privacy, intimacy, assistance, nurturing, and control.

Adult fantasies about the unattainable tend to be more mundane and many people are turned on by power.

Example
I often fantasise about a woman who comes into our office. She is a client, and quite a powerful person. I imagine what it would be like to have sex with her. I can't decide if she would be more feminine in bed or not.

Women's fantasies of being taken away from an ordinary everyday situation are mentioned elsewhere. Fantasies that people use as an antidote to ordinariness in daily life are however somewhat different. The sexual content will obviously vary according to the individual and his own imagination, but a large component of such dreams will be the sensuous and sensual activity that goes on. The individual will build fantasies around the relaxation of inhibitions, and in this there is a correspondence with dreams. Whereas in dreams there is an unconscious relaxing of constraints and taboos in order to have the dreamer aware of the richness of his or her inner life, in fantasy there is a conscious relaxation. In times of sexual difficulty the sharing of fantasies between partners can help to bring new life into a relationship. Equally, during periods of stress within relationships, fantasy can be used quite successfully to relieve tension.

Example

My husband has just had to have an operation which means that sex is not possible for a while. I started thinking back to happy memories. I then turned to fantasising both as to what we would do differently if we were young again, and also to what we will do when he gets better. I don't have so many anxieties now.

Many people use fantasy during the sexual act. It is debatable whether this enhances sex, or whether it is an escape mechanism, or perhaps both. Where the individual fantasises about having sex with someone else other than their partner, there is a kind of displacement going on which is possibly as a means of controlling the situation in some way. It would also seem that this particular activity, especially in women, is a way of maintaining some inner untouchable part that is accessible to no-one but herself.

Following on this theme of sex with someone else other than one's partner, is the fantasy of sex with more than one person at the same time. A threesome is attractive to many people, and this may hark back to the initial triangle between mother, father and baby. Often such a fantasy will reveal the other side of a person's sexuality. If he or she is assertive within a pair there may be passivity in fantasies of threesomes. There is thus a counterbalancing going on. This kind of fantasy can also highlight the need for power or dominance within relationships.

Example

I have a fantasy that my wife and her friend take me to bed with them. We all have sex, but where my wife likes me to be assertive, in my fantasy her friend likes me to be very gentle. I'd really like it both ways.

Indeed, power and dominance within sexual relationships appear to be meaningful components of fantasy both for men and women. Often this does not reach the stage of sado-masochism, but restraint and submission do seem to play a large part, particularly for women. Obscenity ('talking dirty') appears also to be important to many people in using fantasy.

It would be difficult to say that fantasy is necessarily a substitute for the sexual act. Because, as mentioned previously, the individual can work on fantasies and embroider them, they can be used deliberately as emotional and physical relief mechanisms. Sexual dreams, however, arise from suppressed information, and can therefore be more frightening and difficult to understand. It is perhaps easiest to think of dreams being a message from the unconscious, whereas fantasy is manipulating known facts . Dreams are also likely to use symbolism far more, whereas fantasy is more explicit.

SECTION TWO
Sexual Symbolism

The mind has a habit of presenting symbols for consideration in dreams. Symbols are 'a material thing taken to represent an immaterial or abstract concept or idea'. Sexual symbolism is a very rich language, since the various taboos and habits which have grown up around the exploration of the spiritual and sexual worlds draw on many cultures and systems of belief. The dreamer's mind is capable of sifting this huge store of material, and bringing forward the ones which will have most impact for him. Often these symbols are not fully understood until after much consideration.

Concepts such as bisexuality, hermaphrodism, homosexuality and incest - while often being prohibited subjects in conscious waking life - can occur in dreams. They arise as a way of 'shocking' the dreamer into thinking about the balance between his more logical and his more sensitive side. Such dreams do not indicate any type of perversion, but rather a way of understanding oneself.

Frankly sexual acts such as ejaculation, intercourse or kissing will suggest a need for intimacy and the satisfaction of physical needs, or perhaps of coming to terms with old concepts, ideas and beliefs. Other bizarre practices such as fetishism, sadism and masochism often suggest hidden urges which could not and would not be acknowledged in conscious life. These can safely surface and be dealt with in dreams without harming others.

For clarity and ease of reference the entries in this section are arranged in alphabetical order, and cross-referenced.

A - Z

ADULTERY

Abandoned

If, as a child, one had to go into hospital it would not be uncommon to have recurring dreams in adulthood of **being abandoned**. This can lead to problems in forming relationships for fear of being left later. To be abandoned, i.e. **without restraint** -particularly in a sexual way in a dream - may signify that we need to 'loosen up' and be more open in our waking lives. Consciously we will have applied certain morals and restrictions that need not be applied in the dream state. Our capacity for unrestrained fun is increased and initially that behaviour is shocking. If we think carefully about our actions we will recognise a side of our personality which can give us more freedom in our everyday lives.

Abortion

While an abortion may appear to have sexual implications, more properly there may be a need to reject a feeling, emotion, belief or concept which is causing problems within relationships. We have possibly either decided to take a risk with our emotions or have made an abortive attempt to form new relationships which have not worked. We need to make decisions which will get rid of that which is no longer needed in our lives. These can be either past or new ways of behaviour.

Acorn

Since the acorn is a symbol of fertility and abundance, dreaming of one indicates there is a new potential for strength within our lives. There is a huge potential for growth emerging from small beginnings. When looked at in terms of relationships, the acorn symbolises perfect unity - the lower cup represents the female and the rest the masculine.

Adolescent

The dreams which an adolescent has are often exploratory in nature, and give the opportunity to look at the potential in various relationships. To dream of an adolescent will take us back to a time when we were able to be freer and more open in our responses.

Adultery

Dreams of adultery are often connected with our feelings of sexual inadequacy. It may be that at some deep level we

AEROPLANE

need the reassurance that we are still attractive to other people. If we dream of **our partner committing adultery** we may be aware of a problem or difficulty within the partnership which needs resolving.

Aeroplane - See Journey

Affair
Dreaming of an affair allows us to come to terms with our own sexual needs and desires for excitement and stimulation and to be able to release such feelings. We may feel the need to take action which means taking emotional risks. Often to dream of **an affair with someone you hardly know** can reveal an attraction of which you are not consciously aware. Conversely, such a dream can alert you to the type of person you may feel is close to your 'ideal' for the opposite sex. You may be seeking an integration of opposite polarities - male/female, drive/receptivity, good/bad.

Alien
While there are no obvious reasons to disbelieve claims of people having been abducted by space aliens, many such occurrences have a dream-like quality. It has indeed been suggested that apparent events are, in fact, only dreams. Such dreams may contain an element of abuse, whether sexual or otherwise. We all have a need to understand how we can allow ourselves to be abused. An alien appearing in dreams often signifies a part of ourselves which is markedly different from the rest of us and may behave in an unexpected manner.

Amputation
Dreaming of having part of our body amputated often indicates a fear of sexual inadequacy. This is because, in dreams, all appendages can be substituted for the penis. It is thought that this sense is connected with the process of growth which goes on in the womb.

Animals
Suppressed sexual urges can show up in dreams as animals. Many people have dreams about animals and these may represent those parts of ourselves which we suppress in the mistaken belief that we are handling them. Thus **fierce animals** can suggest that we need to pay attention to those aspects of our personality which gives us difficulty. If we

ANIMALS

are **attacked by an animal** it may indicate that we have decided that our sexual response - whether positive or negative - to someone is not appropriate.

Various animals can have differing meanings in dreams of a sexual nature, as may be seen in the following examples:-

Bear The mother appears in dreams in many forms, the bear being one of them. The image may be of the possessive, devouring mother or of the all-caring mother, and relates to how we feel about the mother or mother figure in our lives.

Bull The bull is recognised as sexual passion or creative power.

Cat The feline, sensuous side in human beings, usually in women, is often represented by the cat. In dreams, the cat therefore often denotes the capricious side of the feminine.

Cow The eternal feminine power - especially the mother - is often depicted by the cow.

Dog Dreaming of dogs can often show that a connection is being made with one of the feminine archetypes, that of the Amazon - the self-sufficient woman. Room needs to be made in the dreamer's life for this aspect of femininity, whether the dreamer is male or female.

Domesticated (Tame) animals Dreaming of animals which have been tamed shows that we are aware of those wilder parts of ourselves with which we have come to terms. We all have passions which, although probably never very formidable, are being used in a controlled way.

Goat Dreaming of a goat is to recognise creative energy and masculine vitality and sexuality. A goat can also signify pure lust.

Hare The hare in dreams can be either negative or positive, in that it can represent sexual madness, but also mothering.

Horse/Mare In a man's dream a mare will denote the Anima, a woman, or the whole realm of the feminine. **In a woman's dream**, being kicked by a horse may indicate her desire, or need, for a relationship with a man. Dreaming of a **black horse** shows that the dreamer needs to take note - and be aware - of their passionate nature.

Kangaroo A kangaroo is unusual in that it carries its young after they have been born. In dreams it often stands for the caring, nurturing aspect of motherhood and strength. Dreaming of one can show that the dreamer has a

ANIMALS

need for this in their waking lives.

Monkey The monkey characterises the infantile, childish and arrested side of the dreamer's character. The qualities of mischief, impudence and inquisitiveness all belong to the monkey.

Parts of animals (the limbs, eyes, mouth etc.) have the same significance as parts of the human body. If **the four legs** are particularly emphasised the whole rounded personality with all four functions of the mind fully developed is being highlighted.

Pigs Big litters of piglets can represent fruitfulness, although sometimes without result, since the sow can depict the Destructive Mother.

Rabbit The rabbit is a recognised symbol of fertility.

Ram The ram is a symbol of masculine virility and power.

Reptiles To dream of reptiles indicates that we are looking at the more frightening lower aspects of the personality. We could therefore be easily devoured by them, and may feel we have no control over them.

She-wolf The she-wolf can suggest either a strong mothering instinct or the whore.

Unicorn Dreaming of a unicorn often suggests the control of the ego and selfishness. Traditionally the unicorn could only be owned and perceived by virgins and therefore is a symbol of sexual purity. It is a return to, and a recognition of, an innocence necessary in self-understanding.

Wild Animals There is a destructive force arising from the unconscious and threatening the safety of the individual. Usually wild animals stand for danger, dangerous passions, or dangerous people. Having such a dream may be a way of understanding anxiety.

Anima/Animus

In dreams we are able to make a connection with those parts of ourselves of which we do not normally make use. Where a man may not understand or feel any connection with his feminine side, the part that he is most wary of - often the seductress - will appear in dreams as an unknown and yet very desirable woman. A woman may be attempting to come to terms with the more logical objective side of herself, and need to make a deep connection with her own masculine side. This may be depicted in dreams as a strong protective male to whom she is sexually attracted in the dream scenario (In waking life, after having had a dream which highlights the inner changes, we may actually find ourselves physically attracted to an approximation of the dream figure). Dreaming of a figure of the opposite sex, and highlighting a particular facet of their personality allows us to make a different type of connection with other people in waking life. We can begin to relate to people in such a way that the sexual act in real life can be enhanced. It becomes an appreciation of them rather than simply an act of gratification for ourselves. We also become able to be more objective about ourselves, and therefore more able to see clearly our own part in relationships of all sorts.

Appetite

An appetite can be translated into lust or desire. Such an image or feeling can appear in dreams because we find difficulty in accepting our own basic needs; therefore the subconscious creates something which we can accept as valid. There may also be a lust for life which leads us into experiencing life more fully with all its attendant appetites.

Armour

Emotional rigidity and fear can be shown in dreams as armour; interestingly the type of armour shown can give an inkling of the defences we or others may use. **Old-fashioned armour** may represent old fashioned attitudes, where a **bullet-proof vest** - because it protects the heart area - would suggest fear of being loved. **Chain mail**, by word association, seen in a woman's dream might alert her to a slightly more laissez-faire attitude in her lover. The ideal lover is often concealed from us in dreams by armour of some sort. **If, in a woman's dream she is wearing the armour,** she may have connected with that part of her which protects herself through her faith and religious beliefs. The archetypal figure of Joan of Arc is of great relevance to women, as it encompasses both innocence and passion.

Attack

Any attack in a dream may have sexual connotations since the sexual act is probably when we are at our most vulnerable, both as men and women. It may be that we feel threatened by close proximity with another human being, and have to

ASS

overcome that fear before closeness is possible. There could also be a fear of our own natural urges, perhaps of not being able to control ourselves or others.

Ass

Often the mind will play tricks in the dream state. An image will surface which has an obvious association through its sound with something else. By its similarity to the slang word arse, the ass would suggest our lower sexual urges, and perhaps the genital area. As in Shakespeare's *A Midsummer Night's Dream*, an ass can also represent foolishness in love. The dreamer should look at his feelings about a relationship.

B

Baby - Also see Embryo and People in dreams

For many women there is a biological clock which dictates that at certain times in her life, she wishes to have a baby. This can happen first around the time of puberty when she wants something that belongs entirely to her - almost a doll to look after. It happens again from the late twenties to early thirties, when she becomes conscious of her ability to nurture a child successfully. A third time is also around the mid-forties, when she appreciates that there is little time left for her to give birth successfully. It is often at these times that she will dream of babies, either her own or others. She becomes more conscious through dreams of her ability both to bond with her baby, and to be responsible for it.

Bar

In dreams, the iron bar can sometimes be taken to symbolise the erect penis. It is as though the dreamer cannot accept a direct reference to the penis itself, and therefore creates an acceptable image. For a **man to dream of beating someone with an iron bar** could suggest an inappropriate and violent use of his sexuality. Dreaming of being in **a drinking bar** can show that the dreamer is aware of the transient nature of many relationships and his ability to be open to casual sex.

Bestiality - Also see chapter on Deviations

At the beginning of any programme of self development, we can become aware of dream scenarios which in real life would be totally against our own moral codes. Usually these are representative of a course of action which may be necessary. In this case, bestiality suggests the need to become aware of - and to integrate - the lower, less- developed side of our instinctive behaviour. Often the act is not actually witnessed; it is more the likelihood of such a thing happening which is recognised. It is not that the dreamer is perverted - in fact it is more likely the opposite. He or she is realising that there are different ways of handling sexuality.

Bicycle - See Journey

Birth
The urges to care, to love and to give birth are all suggested by dreams of birth. It may be both a spiritual and a physical need. We will often dream of birth at the beginning of a new relationship, particularly when we are aware of a physical attraction to someone.

Bisexuality
Bisexuality can be depicted in dreams, when the dreamer becomes aware of both the masculine and feminine aspects held within his or her own personality. There is often conflict between these parts, or between the inner and outer selves. This can show itself in dreams as bisexuality and a need for deep relationship with members of both sexes.

Bite/Biting
Biting suggests a degree of aggression, and a hidden desire to hurt. In sexual terms, it is often the desire to suckle in the same way that a baby does. This is so both for men and women, although obviously that need is more easily satisfied for men than for women. Interestingly though, many men are afraid of being eaten. This can be represented in dreams by being bitten by the feminine or a symbol that stands for femininity. It is thought that this is a remnant of an animal instinct, present when the mother will ensure the survival of the fittest by eating the weaker of her young.

Body
Since being 'physical' is the baby's first experience of itself, the body forms the prime source of information.
The lower part of the body represents the instincts and

BODY

emotional aspects of a character. If there is **conflict between the upper and lower part** it indicates that there is disharmony between the mental faculties and instinctive behaviour. Often a sexual difficulty will manifest in dreams as a conflict between the upper and lower parts of the body.

Abdomen, stomach, belly The abdomen is the seat of repressed sexuality and emotions, so to dream of a pain in the stomach could suggest some sexual difficulty.

Arms A passionate commitment can be indicated by a hug or being held.

Breasts Our connection with the mother figure and our need for nurturing is often suggested by a dream of breasts. It also suggests the wish to be without responsibilities, as a baby is, and also the desire to be free and uninhibited.

Constipation can suggest sexual repression, holding onto what we have and not allowing ourselves to let go.

Ejaculation in dreams indicates the need for sexual relief.

Excrement Bodily functions may be seen as dirty and self-centred. **Evacuation of the bowel** in dreams can also signify the sexual act. The connection between excrement and sexuality means that some people still believe that sex is 'not nice'.

Hair The hair - being an extension of the body - can suggest some fear or doubt connected with sexuality. For **a woman to dream of cutting a man's hair** may indicate her fear of his masculinity and her attempt to deal with it.

Limbs Whether it is to do with cellular memory and the growth process that takes place is uncertain, but in dreams any limb can be taken to mean sexuality and fears associated with gender issues. In dreams, any limb can represent the penis. Thus for a **limb to be amputated** suggests a fear of castration.

Mouth Sometimes the mouth can symbolise the feminine side of our nature, particularly the devouring all-encompassing side.

Penis Dreaming of a penis - either one's own or someone else's - usually highlights the attitude to 'penetrative sex'. It will certainly bring into focus the attitude to penetrative sex, and may reveal what the dreamer feels or fears. To interpret a dream of a penis

BODY

depends on whether the dreamer is male or female.

Skin Skin in a dream stands for our persona, or the facade we create for others. Dreaming of **hard, tough skin** indicates that we have created a tough exterior and are trying to protect ourselves. Often a dream of **piercing the skin** suggests the first sexual act that takes away a girl's virginity. The dream image of direct penetration is too difficult to handle and the mind has created an alternative image.

Teeth Popularly, teeth are supposed to stand for aggressive sexuality - although more properly they signify the growth process towards sexual maturity. **If one is anxious about teeth dropping out** it suggests there is a fear of getting old and undesirable. **In a woman's dream, if the teeth are swallowed** this can signify a desire for pregnancy. Generally teeth and the use of them suggest aggressive sexuality, although equally they signify the growth towards sexual responsibility (See **Biting**). **Having the teeth drilled** suggests the sexual act (the drill being the most relevant part). **Having teeth extracted** signifies emasculation and the loss of power. Teeth in a dream will often turn into something else which can be swallowed.

Tongue The tongue often suggests, by displacement, the penis and sometimes sexual temptation. Another explanation that is much more basic is that of the symbolism of the serpent and the phallus, and hence sexuality.

Urine How we deal with urine in dreams often also tells us a great deal about our own sexuality. Because there is a strong connection between the act of voiding urine and ejaculation, one may represent the other in dreams.

Vagina Most often, dreams of the vagina are to do with one's self-image. **In a woman's dream**, it highlights her receptivity. **In a man's dream** it suggests his need to be penetrative, both mentally and physically. Not many people dream directly of the vagina except with relevance to the sexual act, although it can be represented in dreams by dark passages and corridors.

Womb Dreams of **returning to the womb** suggest our need to reconnect with the passive, more yielding side of our nature. It is said there is a wish to return to a state of innocence.

Bottle

In many dreams a bottle can stand for the vagina. What is in the bottle can also be important in understanding the way we handle our own and others' sexuality. **Wine**, for instance, might suggest the intoxicating aspect of sex. **Catching fish or sea creatures** suggests the sexual act itself, and may represent a woman's need for pregnancy. Whether the **bottle is full or empty** may, particularly in a man's dream, suggest his sexual prowess.

Boy - See People in dreams

Boyfriend - See People in dreams

Breasts - Also see Body

For a **man to dream of breasts** usually indicates his unconscious connection with his mother or the nurturing principle. **Sucking the breast** in dreams is a return to the infantile state, where there is no responsibility and all one's needs are met. When a woman becomes conscious of her breasts in a dream, she is concentrating on herself as a woman, and may be ready to take on the responsibility of parenthood.

Bride - Also see Marriage

At its simplest level, dreaming of a bride may be expressing a subconscious need and a desire to be married or to be in a successful partnership. We may also be searching for the innocent feminine within us. There may be issues to do with virginity, particularly if the dreamer is a woman. Psychologically, we are hoping to achieve a union of the unintegrated part of ourselves.

Bridegroom - Also see Marriage

In men, the need for partnership may often be more intellectual than emotional and it may be necessary to make a connection with this particular drive. Unless we have very strong beliefs on marriage, in today's less repressed climate one is less likely to dream of stereotypes such as brides and bridegrooms when there is a strong desire for sexual activity to take place.

Brothel

To dream of a brothel indicates the need for sexual liberation and freedom. If a **woman dreams of being in a brothel**, she may not yet have come to terms with the sexually active, seductive side of herself. She may be aware of her own ability to 'prostitute herself' in some way to make herself available to men. If a **man dreams of being in a brothel** it may show a fear of the feminine. If in waking life he is somewhat promiscuous, he may be considering the way he relates to his own and others' sexuality.

Brutality
When there is brutality in dreams we may be recognising the darker, more animal side of ourselves. It will depend on whether we are being brutally treated, or whether we are the perpetrator. Within the sexual scenario, there may be a sadistic need for a victim. Unrestrained passion - whether sexual or otherwise - can appear as brutality and cruelty in our dreams. We may also be afraid in waking life of hurting others or of being hurt.

Bud
Particularly in teenage dreams, the bud represents emerging sexuality. A flower symbolises femininity, so a bud is more often to do with the dawning realisation of a woman's power. It can also, however, suggest the engorgement of the penis in arousal.

Bull - Also see Animals
The bull represents the masculine principle and fertility, and therefore suggests a more aggressive tenacious kind of sexuality. In dreams the bull can sometimes signify frustration of the sexual urge. That frustration can more often than not come from others around us rather than our own inability.

Bullet
A bullet in a dream has a connection with the idea of sexual impregnation. If the dreamer is male he will have an awareness of his own sexual potency, but also of the need to control his actions. If the dreamer is female there may be unconscious fears and doubts about the sexual act.

Burglar - Also see Intruder
A burglar or intruder in dreams - particularly those which have a strong sexual symbolism - suggests that we are experiencing some form of infringement of our private space. A burglar **in a woman's dream** can also represent the sexual act, particularly when she has not given permission in waking life for intercourse.

C

Candle

A candle in a dream which is sexual in content can have more than one meaning. From its original meaning (control of personal magic), it can suggest sexual potency. It can also be accepted as a symbol of the aroused penis, and as a third meaning can convey lust and desire.

Cane - Also see chapter on Deviation

As a tool which is used for punishment, the cane suggests the deliberate sexual arousal which can be felt through chastisement. This can be either sadistic or masochistic. A cane is also phallic.

Car - See Journey

Castrate

The violent act of castration in a dream indicates the damage we are capable of doing to ourselves in denying our inner fears. In any dream that contains sexual trauma, we are usually being alerted to such fears. Conventionally, there may be some difficulty in coming to terms with the conflict between the masculine and feminine within oneself. Dreaming of castration also suggests that we are prepared to make a life sacrifice, to give up or control the sexual act in favour of celibacy.

Cat

Any member of the cat family appearing in dreams represents the feminine, and often her more devious side. The type of cat will give an indication of which aspect the dreamer is being made aware. For instance, the **panther** represents Lilith (Adam's first partner) and the more destructive side of the feminine. The **tiger** suggests nobility and dignity. If it is man-eating the symbolism is obvious. The **domestic cat** suggests love and healing. The slang word 'pussy' for women's sexual parts can actually be symbolised in dreams as a cat.

Cave

Entering a cave in certain dreams suggests entering - or sometimes leaving - the feminine. As a place of mystery, the cave also represents the dark secret places where we hold our basic instincts. It also shows we can emerge into rational rather than instinctive behaviour.

CLOTHES

Chain
Any type of chain appearing in dreams signifies some form of binding - that is, joining two people or things together. This could be romantically, such as by **ribbons or daisy chains**. In dreams or fantasies where there are **iron chains**, this may suggest bondage and connect with a possibly sadistic or masochistic part of the dreamer's awareness.

Cigar/Cigarette
Particularly **in a woman's dream** a cigar can suggest the penis, and therefore masculinity. It may also suggest the powerful successful male. A cigarette generally being more easily accessible may simply suggest choices which have to be made in dealing with sexual activity.

Clean
Despite the changing attitudes to sex and sexuality many people still make a connection between cleanliness and sexuality. We may have subconsciously inherited such attitudes from our parents. In waking life, an obsession with cleanliness can suggest that the sufferer may not have come to terms with his or her own sexuality in some way.

Climbing
In sexual dreams climbing not only means overcoming obstacles, but also reaching for what might be called 'peak experience'. It ties in with the idea that there is a change in perception and energy during the sexual experience.

Clothes
Clothes are both a cover-up and a statement. They can be used both to protect ourselves against being touched and to disguise our sexuality, or to reveal our vulnerability or sexuality. For instance, if a woman is wearing a very short skirt in a dream when in waking life she would not think of doing so, this would suggest that she is beginning to accept her attractiveness and her sexuality. Being aware of **getting undressed,** particularly when there is someone else present, symbolises the ability to be open and uninhibited in our actions. **A man wearing woman's clothing or a uniform on a woman** highlights a growing awareness of the need for a balance between the masculine and feminine. It does not mean that the dreamer is transvestite. Many articles of clothing can have sexual connotations:-

CLOTHES

Body stocking As women become freer there is less need for them to be cluttered up by their clothes. A body stocking in a dream can therefore suggest a healthy attitude to sexuality, and a woman's awareness of the need for a complete relationship, not just a sexual one.

Hat The hat is an interesting symbol because it can represent both spirituality and sexuality. Nowadays it can, for obvious reasons, suggest safe sex but it can also represent respect.

Pyjamas/Night-clothes Pyjamas suggest ease and hence openness. Night-dresses, if they are long and flowing, suggest the more erotic side of the feminine, although they can be used to symbolise innocence and purity.

Raincoat It will depend very much on who is wearing the raincoat as to the interpretation. The 'dirty raincoat' is easily interpreted. The raincoat may also suggest some lack of development and a wish to return to a womb-like state. Raincoats will often appear in fantasies.

Underclothes Underclothes will often symbolise our underlying feelings about ourselves. In dreams, for instance, we may recognise we are wearing 'sexy' underwear while being outwardly very businesslike, and vice versa.

Veil or veil-like garments When someone is wearing a veil in a dream there is a need to preserve a mystery. This may be the essential mystery of the feminine, or something that the dreamer does not wish to have revealed. Veil-like garments are more likely to suggest the former, where a veil will suggest the latter.

Cock

Often in dreams there is a play on words. A cock may thus be seen as a penis, or may be represented by a cockerel. Many magical rites required the sacrificing of a cockerel - the masculine principle - and this image can surface even in today's sophisticated society.

Constipation

Constipation in a dream suggests a withholding of oneself and therefore, in the sexual sense, the inability to relate properly to someone. It also indicates a fear of sex itself, in the ability to let go and enjoy the act. Often to dream of constipation can suggest that we are holding on to something which may turn bad, and cause us difficulties. In real life constipation can cause piles, which simply makes the problem worse.

D

Dagger
Many sexual dreams contain images of sharp pointed instruments. While a dream may not have an overtly sexual theme, whenever there is such an image it is worthwhile seeing if there is other sexual symbolism. In the dream it may be possible to deal with issues to do with sexuality, in such a way that we can resolve fears and doubts.

Dam
When feelings become overloaded, particularly with regard to sex or sexuality, we may often dream of a dam overflowing or bursting. There is often a feeling of emotional relief and release in waking life following such a dream. Thus, the **bursting of a dam** can also represent an orgasm.

Dance/Dancing
Dancing as a ritualised activity can suggest, in dreams, the foreplay necessary for successful sex. In waking life, dancing creates happiness and possibly intimacy. In dreams, rather than portraying the sexual act, the mind symbolises it as dance. In the animal kingdom 'dance' is an important part of the mating ritual. The male peacock's display is an example of this. The **pace of the dance** often signifies the dreamer's attitude to sex and sexuality. For example, a slow dance such as a waltz would be more romantic than wild, abandoned dancing.

Date
Dreaming of being **out on a date with someone** suggests the beginning of a sexual interest of which we are not yet aware in waking life. We perhaps need to recognise that we are capable of linking romantically with a particular person.
As **a fruit** the date is an ancient symbol of fertility and fertility rites. In everyday life it is supposed to be an aphrodisiac and may have this symbolism in dreams.

Death
Death and sexuality are very closely connected. The dying off of sexual excitement after orgasm is seen by many as a death, and often can be experienced this way in dreams.

DEEP

When intense feelings arise with no appropriate outlet, this can be experienced as a death or a decline. Intense devotion can also give rise to great amounts of hostility, and to enable the dreamer to escape from these feelings there has to be a 'death'. Often this death is simply the death of the old self, in that nothing can ever be the same again. The strong sense of loss which is felt when a relationship comes to an end is often depicted as a death in dreams. After divorce, for instance, many people will dream of the death of their former partner. It is almost as though they need the symbolism of death to allow themselves to grieve. When a young person undertakes a new relationship outside the family circle, he or she will often dream of the death of a parent. This is frequently the only way to for the youngster to break away from the family restrictions. There may then be the need to make changes in all the relationship structures which one has built up. Dreaming of **oneself being dead** alerts us to the fact that we have allowed parts of ourselves to be killed off, perhaps as a compromise for the sake of a new relationship.

Deep
The deep well - or anything that has a great depth to it - suggests the extent of feeling that is possible within any meaningful relationship. We may well have previously repressed our innermost selves, only to have that part set free within a relationship.

Defence
Defence mechanisms are one of the things most often depicted in dreams. These may be symbolised by walls, moats, fences and barriers. The perception that a woman's defences need to be broken down before she is ready for sexual intercourse makes foreplay a necessary part of sexual activity. She will often dream of defences being breached or removed before she is consciously ready for sexual activity. Conversely, a man may also need to be aware of his own defences if he is to relate properly to his partner.

Depression
One of the most commonly recognised causes of depression is a breakdown in relationships; dreams will often attempt to compensate for this. At a time when we consciously do not feel like any sexual activity at all,

dreams will create occasions for such activity that simply makes the waking situation hard to deal with. We may dream of having sex with our former partner, or even a previous partner.

Desert
A desert, being a barren land, may actually represent barrenness in the sense of being without, or unable to have, children. This symbol often appears in women who are reaching the menopause. It is important to realise that this is a state of mind rather than a physical reality. A desert can also signify isolation, although this state may also contain within it a potential for growth.

Devil
The Devil is frequently a representation of feelings and desires that we do not understand or of which we are afraid. It is often the wilder, more pagan side of ourselves. Because the conventional figure with horns and a tail is so well known, it becomes a symbol of all that we may consider evil. In dream terms, therefore, it can represent the basic drive towards sexual activity.

Devour
Dreams in which the dreamer is being devoured indicate one of two things. We are all fearful of being consumed, whether by our own passions, or of being taken over by someone else. Our love or feelings can become all-consuming, and be very threatening either to ourselves or others.

Displacement
Displacement activity occurs when we are not able to face whatever reality we have created. We will get cross with the cat rather than angry at our boss. In dream scenarios, displacement will often occur when our subconscious minds cannot accept a particular reality. So, for example, dreaming of **putting something in a bag** can represent sexual activity or becoming pregnant; **catching a bus** can represent how we relate to people we work with or to groups that we know.

Divorce
The trauma of divorce often sparks off dreams that try to deal with the perceived problems that may often be sexual in origin. Whether the dreamer is masculine or feminine, their perception of themselves is bound to be lessened. Lack of self-esteem often causes us to

doubt our ability to handle a successful relationship at all. Many of the doubts and fears that occurred during the teenage period may well resurface at this time.

To dream of actually **being divorced** touches our fear of being left alone. It is not unusual for the partner of someone who is terminally ill to dream of being divorced from that person. This is often an attempt on the part of the dreamer to come to terms with the forthcoming loss. An extreme sense of loneliness occurring when the dreamer is divorced - or about to be so - can be translated in dream image into drowning or being buried.

Dragon
A dragon in dreams can represent unrestrained passion or an overbearing person. In dreams about taming a dragon the interpretation will depend on whether the dreamer is male or female. If female, it generally represents overcoming her own fears and doubts, particularly in the sexual arena. If male, it is to do with subduing feminine passion.

Driving - See Journey

E

Earthquake
An earthquake in dreams can suggest extreme emotion and also the upheaval that is caused on a psychological level by a new relationship or sexual activity. It can represent anything from a gentle turbulence to a complete breakdown of previously held ideas and ideals.

Eating
Hunger, like sex, is a basic drive. **To be eating** something in a dream shows the need to satisfy this hunger. Sexual need arises later in life than hunger, and the latter can be substituted for the less well understood one of sexual satisfaction. It will often depend on **what is being eaten** as to how the dream is interpreted. Foods with an aphrodisiac quality may alert us to our inner needs.

Eclipse
Dreaming of an eclipse or a blotting out of the sun highlights a very old fear which many men have of emasculation and of losing their power to a woman. For **the moon to be eclipsed** would

suggest the disempowerment of the feminine, and on a very deep level, an awareness of her unpredictability.

Egg
The egg is a symbol of new life and new beginnings. In dreams it can suggest the beginning of a new relationship, either sexual or otherwise. Principally it depicts the coming together of two entities in order to create a third being. It can therefore represent the result of sexual activity.

The egg is also a symbol of perfect life, and unless we are completely closed off from the world we live in, is the realisation of the massive potential of everything which we are. A new relationship can make us aware in a way hitherto not possible of just what our potential really is.

Example
One dreamer dreamt he laid an egg (his potential) in the sea (his emotional self) which grew into a new world. His girlfriend in waking life later introduced him to the world of classical music, which he grew to love.

Ejaculation
To be having sex in a dream and to take that dream to the point of ejaculation is nothing of which to be ashamed. It simply suggests that the dreamer is aware of the necessity to satisfy his sexual needs in an appropriate way. There is within each of us the ability to 'express' our desires fully if we can only give ourselves that permission. Dreaming of ejaculation suggest we have done just that. We are then able to give up old ideas and beliefs that are no longer valid.

Often in sleep there are various physiological changes that will take place - one of which is a spontaneous erection. This may be interpreted in dreams as ejaculation. Also spontaneous ejaculation may occur, particularly at puberty and other times of change.

Eloping/Elopement
As mentioned elsewhere many women fantasise about being carried away by the man of their dreams. To dream of eloping firstly indicates a need to escape from a difficult situation, secondly suggests conflict with some kind of authority figure, and thirdly highlights the fact that we are prepared to risk a great deal for love. When

the **person we are eloping with is known** to us we are most likely aware of our mutual need to escape. **If the person is unknown** we may need to tackle a part of our personality that we have not yet recognised. Our motives may be to integrate that part of our personality away from prying eyes. In today's climate, where parental pressure is no longer quite so restrictive, elopement would be more likely to represent trying to escape from old values and beliefs about ourselves.

Embryo - Also see Baby

Dreaming of an embryo or foetus is very different from dreaming of an actual baby. A baby is fully formed, whereas an embryo is not capable of sustaining life on its own. Therefore, in dreams which have a sexual content to them, an embryo would suggest a relationship that is not yet fully formed. We may feel that it will not survive unless energy is put into it from both parties in the relationship. It may also suggest a vulnerable part of ourselves which needs nurturing and surrounding with loving care until such times as it is able to survive on its own.

Emission

The images that arise in dreams prior to orgasm will often reveal the dreamer's feelings about sex. Conflicts that arise can frequently be dealt with by dreaming of orgasm and emission.

Emotions

Emotions in dreams can become very intense, and perhaps more extreme than those we allow ourselves to experience in everyday life. For instance, we may be a little attracted to someone in real life, only to find that we are obsessive about them in dreams. This is because dreams allow us to link with our inner selves and give us a means of understanding ourselves which would not be available to us in any other way. The dream scenario will often allow us free expression, and the swings of mood that are associated with loving and sexual activity may become understandable in the context of the dream. Sometimes when we do not understand our own emotions we can experience one of our dream characters showing the same emotion, and this allows us to be objective about ourselves. An example might be dreaming of a husband and wife, where the husband experiences sadness because his wife wishes to leave him. The dreamer has ambivalent feelings as to whether he should leave his partner.

Our dreams can also be affected by our emotions in everyday life. For instance, to dream of **being with a lover in a beautiful garden** would highlight our good feelings about ourselves, whereas to be **on a stormy sea** would suggest a turbulent relationship.

Engine

The sexual impulse or instinctive drives and one's basic motivation are all symbolised by the engine.

Explosion

An explosion can obviously represent an orgasm. It is a forceful release of energy that creates change, that change being inevitable. If the emotion behind the explosion is experienced as being negative - for instance, rage or impotence - there can be an element of destruction which needs to be understood. If, however, the build-up of energy is positive, then it will result in pleasure and relaxation. Dreaming of such an explosion can provide a safe space to explore our own reactions to such a sexual release.

F

Failure

Fear of failure is one of the biggest anxieties which anyone has, and because it is so basic to human nature, it can manifest itself in dreams in many ways. Dreaming of **having sex with someone and finding that one is impotent** does not necessarily mean that in real life this is so. It is more likely to mean that one fears being helpless in a particular situation. Failure to reach an orgasm in waking life can appear as other types of failure in dreams. **Failing to communicate** with a partner in a dream can highlight a degree of sexual frustration. **Failure to recognise someone or something** in dreams can suggest that there is an aspect of our lives or conduct we do not wish to confront.

Fairies

Fairies, gnomes, elves, nymphs and dryads are all representations of elemental forces. When they appear in dreams, particularly those with any sexual content or symbolism, they signify those qualities in us which give us access to the more capricious side of ourselves. They link with the basic forces of earth, fire, air and water and all the energies that they suggest. Since in slang terms a 'fairy' is a derogatory term for a homosexual male, there could also be a type of word play here. This of course does not suggest that the dreamer is, or will be, homosexual.

Falling

In sexual dreams falling mostly suggests surrender or submission. Whether this is sexually submitting by a woman - or the giving up of previously held defences - depends on the personality of the dreamer. Falling can equally suggest a lack of confidence, or the idea of being tempted and falling into temptation. We may be put into a position where we must go deep into our own subconscious in order to understand our own sexuality. In fantasy, falling may suggest our ability to let go and give in to trying to get away from the real world.

Family - See People in Dreams

Fat

Often **becoming fat** in a dream will be a similar sort of defence mechanism to that used in everyday life. We would rather cover up our sexuality than learn how to use it properly. It may be that by getting bigger we are able to assimilate more without being hurt. Getting or **being fat** in a dream may also indicate pregnancy.

Flail

The flail (like the whip) is an instrument of punishment, but also has the potential for sexual arousal. Thus **in a man's dream** if he is using the flail it can suggest the sexual act, whereas **in a woman's dream** it will signify submission - whether her own or someone else's.

Fig, Fig Tree or Pipal

Ever since the time of Adam and Eve the fig has been associated with sexuality, fertility, masculinity and prosperity. Dreaming of one shows that we are able to be in touch with all the finer aspects of ourselves. Because of its now known vitamin content, it is generally accepted as both an aphrodisiac and also a food for the soul or more spiritual self.

Fetish

In dreams a fetish can highlight

fear, immaturity and lack of capability. It is a fixation on an external object or action such as a shoe, a piece of clothing and sometimes a ritual without which there can be no sexual activity. There is some evidence that at the unconscious level the individual would prefer a life of chastity. This suggests that if he is able to project his attention elsewhere he is not responsible for his own sexual acts.

Film

In many dreams we adopt the position of observer. To dream of **being at the cinema** acknowledges that there is a part of ourselves which needs careful appraisal. To dream that we are **watching pornographic films** can suggest that we are aware of our ability to be voyeuristic - to take pleasure in other people's sexual activity. Viewing films may suggest, however, that we are not able to handle our own sexuality particularly well, that it is somewhat removed from us. We may also be choosing to live in a reality which is not of our own making. To be **making a pornographic film** suggests we may actually have come to terms with the sexuality which we have, but are still not entirely happy with the reality we are creating. There is perhaps further work which needs to be done. **Starring in such a film** means we recognise that our love lives and sexual activity are being directed by someone else.

Fish - Also see Salmon

In dreams, fish - like tadpoles - often symbolise pregnancy. They can also suggest a new beginning, relationship or new life.

Floating

Floating in dreams often occurs during the teenage years and at times of great change. By being able to relax completely we put ourselves in touch with a different vibration within ourselves. This may be a sexually oriented part, but may also be the more spiritual self. There is an inherent need for freedom.

Flogging

Flogging is likely to belong to the realm of fantasy rather than dreams. **Flogging ourselves** suggests a kind of masochism in our own personality. **Flogging someone else** in dreams or fantasies suggests a suppressed aspect of sadism which we are able to express through dreams, which we would not care to do in everyday life. All feelings which we curb because of the taboos and strictures of modern society can surface in dreams with some violence.

Food

Food in dreams can represent both sensuality and sexuality. Many foods are phallic in shape, while others are noted for their texture. For example, to be **eating a cream cake** might suggest the sensuousness of the sexual act. **To be being fed** in dreams takes us back to babyhood and suggests all the loving and nurturing which we received at that time.

Forest

The forest in symbolism indicates a threshold or a place of testing and initiation. In dreams with a sexual content it indicates entering the mysterious part of ourselves which is feminine. We can come to terms with and understand the more intuitive, emotional and sensitive side of ourselves, and of those around us. The hero in the enchanted forest must either overcome his own fears or die. This is a rather romantic explanation of a man's innate fears of being overcome by the feminine, which he carries right from his first encounter with his mother. The struggle is to survive despite the feminine and then to gain co-operation from this mysterious thing. **In a woman's dream**, the forest is her own ability to protect herself. In one version of the story of Rapunzel, after she escapes by her own efforts from her tower, both she and her prince wander separately through the forest until they find one another.

Frog - Also see Tadpole

The frog in dreams is seen as a representation of the growth towards both sexual and emotional security. Starting with the tadpole, the frog mirrors the growth pattern of the baby in the womb; through its various transformations it also highlights emotional growth. From being protected by the jelly-like frog spawn, it grows and feeds upon its own protective covering until it is mature enough to live in the world unaided. When it has grown sufficiently it can live both on land and in water. This mirrors the human ability to belong to the world, but also to handle emotional issues which arise. The frog is a symbol of fertility and eroticism, and of our ability to transform base energy into something live and vibrant.

G

Garden
In dreams the garden is always a symbol of the feminine. An **enclosed garden** suggests the private defended space which all women try to preserve, and can also suggest virginity. It represents the inner life and self-awareness which is every woman's right. Whether the garden is cultivated or not will suggest different elements of the personality. A **wild garden** would suggest a wilder untamed side to the character, whereas a **well-ordered, well-stocked** garden suggest an organised personality.

Garlic
Because of its shape and its many parts, garlic is often seen as a symbol of fertility. Its pungent smell means that it acts as a protector. It prevents people getting too close, and in dreams may often appear as a protection against a problematic relationship. Through its association with magic it protects against attack when worn, and therefore can be seen to protect against the penetrative act.

Gate
In dreams gates are a symbol of entry and can thus suggest the sexual act. The interpretation depends on whether they are shutting something out or in. **Shutting out** would suggest defence against sex, whereas **shutting in** is protecting one's sexuality. One is active and the other passive. The object of our desire is in any case not yet available to us. **Opening a gate** can suggest the taking of virginity. When there are **four gates** they represent the qualities of sensing, thinking, feeling and intuition. All these are needed in successful relationships.

Girl - See People in dreams

Girlfriend - See People in dreams

Goblet
The goblet is probably one of the oldest symbols to appear in dreams. Because it is a hollow vessel it is taken to represent the feminine in its receptive principle. It also suggests the fullness and sustenance which are available to us through the sexual act, but further suggests the purity and innocence of a truly loving act. Because of its association with legend,

GENITALS

particularly that of the Holy Grail, a goblet also represents the bravery of the masculine in response to the urges from the feminine. That feminine may be part of himself or an external challenge, but it must be overcome if he is to win his lady.

Genitals

When we dream of genitals it is perhaps wise to look at our feelings about our own sensuality and sexuality. For instance, if **a woman dreams of having masculine genitals** it would suggest that she needs to be aware of her own drives. Conversely, a **man dreaming of female genitals** needs to understand his softness and sensitivity. **Dreaming of someone with no genitals** means the recognition of a lack of sexuality or sexual feelings. Interestingly, such a dream could also indicate either a relationship which is truly spiritual in its nature or one where lust has died. If **we dream of mutilated genitals** we may be aware of either our own or someone else's abuse. This may not necessarily be physical or sexual, although it often is of remembered pain.

Gun - Also see Shot and Weapons

The gun or pistol traditionally represents male sexuality. When a woman dreams of being shot, she either wishes - or fears - some kind of sexual aggression. In a man's dream, shooting the gun would suggest some kind of aggressive sexual act. If the dreamer is shooting the gun, it shows that we may be using the masculine side of ourselves in an assertive way in order to defend ourselves.

H

Hall/Passages

The vagina or the anus can be symbolised in dreams as a passage or hallway. For instance, if someone is standing in the hallway in a dream it may signify that we are aware of having allowed someone to penetrate our personal space. This could obviously represent being open to physical penetration, and therefore the sexual act.

Handcuffs

In dreams with a sexual content, handcuffs - or indeed any type of restraint - obviously tie in with all aspects of bondage. Often the dreamer can be excited or stimulated by resistance and power, so in cases where **the dreamer is handcuffed**, it is his or her own resistance that needs to be understood. This may arise from a fear of the sexual act, a fear of the person concerned, or even a fear of their own reaction. Many people have a secret wish to be overcome or forced to submit, and in dreams it is safe to have this happen. If in dreams we are **putting handcuffs on someone** we are aware of our power over someone else.

Harem
It is said that every man desires group sex at some time or another in his life. A harem appearing in a dream will allow him to consider such a thing in safety. Equally, when he becomes aware of the complexities of the feminine nature, he is, through such a dream, able to consider the many aspects of femininity which are presented to him. This can help him to decide what constitutes an ideal sexual partner. **When his mother appears in a dream of a harem** he may be trying to come to terms with her sexuality, rather than his own. **For a woman to dream of being in a harem** suggests that she is understanding her own flamboyant nature, and is also recognising her sensuality. Such a dream may also touch in with the idea that she is just one of many, and not a unique being.

Harness
Often through dream images we become aware of the need for restraint and control. As we become aware of the greater potential we have available to us, we are able to touch in to the wilder side of our personality. We are also able to create circumstances that enable us to make good use of the energy available.

Hermaphrodite
When in waking life we have uncertainties about our ability to play out the roles expected of our gender, we may dream of a hermaphrodite. We cannot determine whether the person is male or female and therefore in our dream scenario have difficulty in deciding what our appropriate reaction should be. As we learn more about ourselves we work towards a balance between the logical and the sensitive sides of ourselves, and sometimes this can be read in a dream as hermaphrodism. This dream may also highlight an aspect of bisexuality.

HOMOSEXUALITY

Homosexuality - Also see chapter on Homosexuality

We may find ourselves attracted to someone of the same sex in dreams because we are actually looking for parental love. Conflict or anxiety about our own gender can also cause us to dream of having intercourse with somebody the same sex as ourselves. We may also be looking for love of a different sort - a nurturing rather than sexual love.

Very often, to dream of a homosexual affair is an attempt to come to terms with differing aspects of ourselves. It leads us to understand that, by integrating a part of ourselves which may have been suppressed in childhood or puberty, we are making ourselves more whole. We are therefore more able to go onto successful relationships of any sort. It does not mean that one is homosexual, simply that there is some mental confusion.

Honey

As a food, honey is supposed to be an aphrodisiac and in ancient history was thought to be the food of the gods. Dreaming of honey therefore suggests power and fertility.

Horns

The god Pan, who represents sexuality as well as life force, wore horns. Thus, horns appearing in dreams hark back to the idea of the animal in the human. A horn also represents the penis and masculinity. For instance, a dream of **a rhinoceros at full charge** would suggest aggressive masculinity. (In Chinese medicine, rhinoceros horn is reputed to be an aphrodisiac.) Because a horn is penetrative, it can also suggest the desire to hurt. Protection is also a quality of horns since the male animal will use his horns to protect his territory. Horns appearing in a dream suggest superiority, either earned or conferred. In Pagan times, as well as in some tribes today, the donning of horns signifies a particularly senior position within the tribe. They were supposed to bestow the power of the animal on the wearer. This is possibly because of their association with masculine power.

Hot

To dream of **being hot** indicates warm passionate feelings. Pleasure can be translated in dreams to a physical feeling. Experiencing **something as hot** that should be cold - e.g. ice - indicates that we are perhaps having difficulty, and experiencing confusion, in sorting out our feelings. Occasionally extreme emotion is interpreted as a physical feeling - so anger, jealousy or other such feelings can be experienced as heat. To be conscious of the fact that our **surroundings are hot** indicates that we are loved and cared for.

Hunt/Huntsman

Since chase and capture are an integral part of the sexual game, dreaming of **being hunted** is mostly taken to be to do with one's sexuality. The part of ourselves that can be sexually destructive and vicious is the part that is often seen as the huntsman.

Hurricane

A hurricane can represent the power of our own passion, or passionate belief, which carries us away. We may feel we are being swept along by circumstances - or possibly someone's passion. We may not know how to handle the results of that passion, and feel it could be disastrous for others. When we experience a hurricane in a dream, we are sensing the force of an element in our lives which is beyond our control - and we are powerless to resist.

I

Incest - See chapter on Deviations

Individuation

Often at times of transition - for instance, from childhood to puberty, and from puberty to adulthood - the individual may have some very sexual and erotic dreams. Individuation is the term given by psychologists to the process which gives rise to those dreams which one goes through as one moves towards maturity.

Injection

Whenever it appears in a dream that **we are being given an injection** we need to look at two meanings. The first is that of needing to be healed, but the second is more important within the framework of the sexual act. When someone penetrates the personal space, we have a choice of co-operating or not. If a **woman is willingly receiving an injection** in a dream this may suggest a desire for a serious sexual relationship or pregnancy. **If she is unwilling** it could suggest a fear of penetration or of sex.

INTERCOURSE

Sometimes, **for a man, being given an injection** might suggest a degree of homophobia.

Intercourse (or heavy petting) The need for intimacy and closeness is an integral part of every human being. In dreams, intercourse can signify this aspect of our being, or sometimes the integration of a part of our personality that we may have denied.

Intruder - Also see Burglar
When we dream of an intruder there are obvious connections with sex and threats to one's sexuality. As human beings, we are very conscious of our own personal space, and to be dreaming of an intruder suggests that we are feeling threatened in some way. Often in dreams the intruder is masculine, and this generally indicates a need to defend ourselves from our own negative responses.

J

Jewellery
Jewellery indicates love given or received. For **a woman to be giving a man jewellery** in her dream suggests that she is attracted to him and perhaps is able to make a gift of her own sexuality and self-respect. **Costume jewellery** which masquerades as something valuable suggests that feelings we initially thought were deep and meaningful are now no longer so. We recognise that an attraction is passing.

Journey
When we discover in dreams that we are on a journey, we are recognising how we handle various elements of our lives. Our drives, aggressions, fears and doubts are all reflected in our **driving,** particularly in dreams. These drives most often arise from the unconscious and express themselves sexually. If we are **driving a vehicle** we are in control of our own urges. If **we are not happy when someone else is driving** we may not trust that person. When **someone else takes over** from us we are becoming passive within a relationship. When **we are overtaken while driving,** we may recognise that our feelings are not being given the respect they deserve.

Passenger It will depend on whether **we are a passenger** in a vehicle or **are carrying passengers**. Being a passenger in a dream when there is sexuality involved suggests our potential for passivity in such a situation. **Travelling with**

JOURNEY

one other **passenger** suggests we may be considering a relationship with that person, or that they are of particular importance in our lives. If they are not clearly shown, it indicates that we are ready for new relationships.

Road The road in a dream suggests our own individual way forward in fulfilling our needs. An **obstacle in the road** will suggest difficulties. **Turns in the road** may indicate a change of direction, whereas **turning back** shows the need to relive a situation, while a **cul-de-sac** would signify the need not to rush headlong into a situation without due care. A cul-de-sac can also represent contraception.

Traffic accidents and offences Our sexuality or self-image may alert us to the fact that we are about to make mistakes within relationships. A **collision** might suggest a conflict with someone. **Road rage** would signify not being in control of our emotions or a relationship which is extremely intense.

Aeroplane An aeroplane in a dream, because of its shape, could be considered to be phallic. Particularly in a woman's dream it can indicate that she is ready to undertake a new relationship. **An airman or pilot** is a romanticised picture of the inner masculine or of the Self.

Bicycling This suggests youth and freedom, and perhaps the first stirrings of sexual awareness. A bicycle in a dream represents a unification of the duality within us. By bringing the two parts of ourselves together we are able to move into a more successful relationship.

Car (or carriage, cart, chariot) How the dreamer handles life is reflected by the car in dreams. A **sporty car** such as a Porsche would suggest a racy personality, whereas a more **comfortable saloon** type suggests a personality that is at ease with itself. In waking life, cars can have a phallic symbolism and can be seen as a reflection of a person's self-image, and possibly their sexuality. Any part of the car will have significance in a dream. An **engine which will not start** may suggest impotence. The **back tyres** might suggest the dreamer's backside, the **steering wheel** the way we control our lives and so on. If the **brakes are not working** we are not exercising proper control over our lives.

Motorbike, motorcycle In dreams a motorcycle is an image of independent behaviour, and often a symbol for the sexual act. It is also a symbol of masculine youth and daring and can be a symbol of freedom. Dreaming of a **Hell's Angel** would suggest the dreamer feels the need for some kind of anarchical behaviour.

K

Key

A key in a dream represents a 'way in' and therefore has come to represent the penis. In dreams where the key is important it is worth looking at whether it represents the masculine.

Kiss

A kiss in a dream, as in waking life, suggests sealing a kind of pact with someone else. We are often about to embark on a new relationship when we dream of a kiss. If we are **being kissed** then we are being acknowledged for who we are.

Knife - Also see Stab and Weapons

A knife appearing in a dream can suggest the cutting off or severing of a relationship. **In a man's dream** a knife can often appear when there is a fear of emasculation or castration. **In a woman's dream** it shows she may either be aware of her own power or be afraid of the act of penetration. She may also be aware of her fear of masculine violence.

Knob

Since many people still have difficulty in calling 'private parts' by their correct name, a knob appearing in a dream can represent the penis or, if the dreamer is a man, his masculinity. The knob can also suggest the sexual act, particularly if it grows bigger in the dream.

L

Lagoon, lake - Also see Water

A lake symbolises the unconscious side of us which encompasses the inner world of feeling and fantasy. It is a rich source of power when it is accessed and understood. If the **lake is contaminated** we may believe we have assimilated ideas and concepts which are not necessarily good for us. A **clear stretch of water** would indicate that we have clarified our fears and feelings about ourselves. The lagoon represents femininity - particularly the darker aspects - and this image will appear in dreams when we lose our fear of that part of our personality. It is often thought to be the home of the magical feminine and of

MASTURBATION

monsters.

Lance

A lance, being a sharp pointed object, symbolises masculine penetrative energy and therefore the phallus. A **surgical lance,** often used to release pus, indicates the releasing of negative energy and therefore has significance as an agent of healing. Putting these two meanings together suggests the idea of 'sexual healing' being available to the dreamer. A **lance of light** can indicate the phallic aspect of solar power, and thus also its potential destructiveness.

Lead/Leading

Dreaming of a dog lead symbolises the connection between our animal natures and our higher self. There is a belief that we can access God just as easily through understanding our own animal nature and instinctive urges as through any philosophical system. **To have lost the dog lead** would indicate a loss of control and perhaps a fear of relationships which cause us to reveal our basic instincts.

Leather

Leather can be connected with sadistic methods of torture, and thus can become connected with sexual behaviour. Leather in dreams often gives an ambivalent message in that it creates a macho image, but also affords protection against penetration. It can also suggest self-flagellation.

M

Marriage/Wedding

A marriage or wedding usually signifies a union which has been made. This may be in waking life and indicate the beginning of a new relationship. It may also suggest the integration of the inner masculine and feminine and the ability to be a whole individual able to access different aspects of oneself.

Masochism - Also see chapter on Deviations

In dreams this may be a hidden desire to be a martyr, or to suffer. It may also stress the necessity to feel extreme emotion.

Masturbation

The act of masturbation in dreams is significant in terms of the need for self-arousal, whether sexual or otherwise. It usually suggests, quite straightforwardly, the need for a different type of stimulation in everyday waking life. It is as though the dreamer is aware that he or she is capable of doing whatever is necessary on their own.

Mattress
A mattress in a dream which has sexual connotations indicates the way that we handle our own sexuality. Therefore, a **soft mattress** would indicate we are comfortable with it, whereas a **hard and lumpy mattress** may show that we find it an uncomfortable thing to deal with.

Maypole
A maypole represents masculine fertility and is one of the original phallic symbols. Recognising the 'dance' that is performed by the Morris men suggests the intricate patterns which are woven during sexual courtship and worship. For a maypole to appear in dreams suggests an awareness both of masculine fertility and also the productiveness offered by the earth itself. This symbolism comes from a time when man was much closer to nature than he is now.

Menstruation
For a woman to be menstruating in a dream can be ambivalent in meaning. It can suggest her defence against the sexual act or her acceptance of her own sexuality and desire to conceive. In this day and age, when men are learning to be more sensitive to feminine needs, for a man to be aware of menstruation in a dream suggests an ability to be aware of his own feminine side. Many of the taboos surrounding sex are breaking down and understanding hormonal changes is one of these. Men are often subconsciously aware of aspects of relationships before they allow themselves conscious knowledge.

Mermaid, merman
Mermaids and mermen are - mythologically - the masculine and feminine representations of the way we link with the emotional inner self (which we do not necessarily understand) and our ordinary everyday conscious self. There are numerous stories of people attempting to mate or link with these creatures of the sea, and usually it is necessary for the mermaid or merman to be human during the day and its own more secret self at night. This highlights an ability to be both deeply emotional and openly conscious. Until these two separate parts are properly inte-

grated, the human being will not be able to survive fully in either reality. In dreams this demonstrates how difficult it is to integrate the two sides of our nature.

Milk
Men apparently require a greater proportion of liquid nourishment than women, while women's intake of solid food is greater. Milk in dreams can suggest semen. Thus, **to be handed a glass of milk** in a dream can suggest the sexual act.

Mirror
In dreams **looking at oneself in a mirror** can suggest a type of narcissism which may be autoerotic or homosexual. There is a creativity which arises out of contemplation of the self. This allows us to create from an inner space those relationships which we need to live our lives as fully as we can. Often a mirror will represent the unconscious self in us. So, to be **watching ourselves in a mirror carrying out a sexually orientated act**, when in fact we would shudder at using a mirror in such a way in waking life suggests that perhaps we should be considering our deepest motivations and feelings. The unconscious may use this image to reassure the dreamer that he is capable of achieving the relationship he sees mirrored.

Miscarriage
A miscarriage may be a more common symbol in a woman's dream because she is more emotionally involved in the process of conception and all its attendant possibilities. To dream of a miscarriage will often indicate that something is not quite right either in herself or in the relationship she is in. As a pregnant woman accustoms herself to the fact that her life will inevitably change, she may dream of a miscarriage as representing those aspects of her life which she must give up. If a woman has already had a miscarriage or a termination, dreaming of a miscarriage may give her the opportunity to grieve. In a man's dream a miscarriage can suggest a fear of fatherhood.

Moat
Often in dreams a moat suggests the defences we use to protect ourselves against intimacy and sexual activity. Sometimes a **dry moat** suggests emotional barrenness. A **moat which is overfull** suggests emo-

tional overflowing.

Motorbike - See Journey

Mud
Sex for some people may still be viewed as dirty. Mud in dreams has a sexual meaning if, for instance, the limbs (which are said to represent the penis) are covered in mud or are being pulled in and out of it. This reproduces the pumping action which occurs during sexual intercourse.

N

Nail
All sharp objects tend to have some significance in sexual symbolism. Dreaming of **woodworking nails** suggests penetrative power. This may be significant if the dreamer is having difficulty with issues of masculinity or sexuality. In waking life being **scratched by fingernails** can, for some, be a highly erotic experience. In dreams it can signify wild behaviour.

Naked/Nude
Nakedness in dreams is a return to the innocent state where everything can be revealed. There is no longer any need for pretence in an intimate situation, and the dreamer can be open and frank. While this will make him vulnerable, it is not something that the dreamer cannot handle. To be **lying naked with someone** suggests a need to understand one's own inner urgings and longings. The dreamer is at a point where natural sexuality is revealed in safety. He or she can drop the inhibitions that have caused difficulty up until now, and be their own true self. If **people in the dream disapprove of nakedness** we are being alerted to the fact that we are allowing others to affect our self-image. Being naked in a dream may simply reveal an underlying prudery that will have to be handled.

Needle
A needle in a dream can suggest masculine sexuality. It can also suggest the need to 'repair' a relationship.

Nightmare
Nightmares arise from an inner conflict that often has its origin in sexual desires which are repressed or denied. Fear and repression go hand in hand, and it is often the fear which surfaces and changes an erotic dream into something

OBJECTS

that has nightmare qualities. Almost inevitably nightmares highlight the dreamer's need to escape either from a person, a thing or a situation. Once the fear is identified in waking life it can usually be recognised as guilt. This is the guilt of having inappropriate desires, fear of impotence, difficulty with sexual expression, or even anxiety over self-approval. Often an incestuous desire can surface as impotence. When in a nightmare there is pressure on the chest or a difficulty in breathing, this may hark back to the process of birth, and therefore be a passive surrender to a stronger power.

Nut
When **nuts and screws** appear in a dream it frequently indicates our need to get down to basics. A nut is considered to be feminine, and the screw masculine. Nuts, as in **Brazil nuts,** etc., have a connection with masculine sexuality and fertility. This is partly to do with their shape, but also because of their aphrodisiac food connection. Dreaming of nuts may suggest that we are trying to de-personalise issues to do with sexuality.

Nymphs
The nymph in dreams most closely approximates to the carefree, fun-loving child within woman. She is the representative of movement and light, and often appears as a princess type of personality. She is difficult to catch and keep hold of.

O

Oats
Wild oats obviously have a connection in people's minds with sexual satisfaction and freedom. To dream of **sowing grain** suggests that we are expecting to reap a benefit from a situation at a later date.

Objects
Relationships and sexual fantasies become easier to deal with and less embarrassing if seen in terms of objects. **Objects that are alive** suggest memories of past relationships which are still alive in the dreamer and playing a part in his life. **Long, oblong, pointed objects; or anything that expands, penetrates, collapses, squirts, ejects; or any objects resembling the phallus** (poles, pens, hose, rope) represent the phallus. **A broken pencil** can rep-

87

resent castration. **Hollow or circular objects, containers and vessels of any kind** (bags, cups, caves) represent female genitalia and therefore the womb, or feminine nature - especially the mother or mother archetype. **A cup or goblet** suggests the whole feminine personality. **Two cups** can indicate the contrast between the positive and negative aspects of motherhood, and equally can be a symbol for the breasts. **Objects coming to life** indicate new life, and new potential developing within the dreamer.

Obscenity

Often dreams will link with the lower, more basic aspects of ourselves. Apparent obscenity in dreams is connected with our perception of ourselves. There may be a part of us of which we do not approve. If we are **performing obscene acts**, we need to be aware of suppressed impulses. If such acts are **performed against us**, we need to decide how we are being victimised in our daily lives.

Obsession

Obsession is an unnatural focusing on a feeling, belief or object. In dreams it can alert us to an inappropriate attraction.

Organ

The various **organs of the body** can represent the different aspects of the self. In dreams they can signify various weaknesses and strengths. In slang terms, the organ suggests the penis.

Orgy

An orgy relates to a tremendous release of energy that can take place when we give ourselves permission to access our own sexuality. This permission will often be given subconsciously at first, and can be expressed in dreams more fully than we would allow ourselves to do in everyday life.

Often our dreams will express a difficulty or blockage we may have in any one area of our lives. Since most people's self image is very much connected with their sexuality, dreaming of an orgy can indicate that appreciation from our peer group can release the blocked energy.

Oven

As a hollow object, in dreams an oven can also represent the womb. With its ability to change ingredients into something else, the oven can also represent the process of gestation and birth.

PEOPLE IN DREAMS

Oyster
The oyster is, by repute, an aphrodisiac food. In dreams it can therefore represent the sexual act or anything associated with sex.

P

Pain
Pain in dreams which have a sexual content to them usually suggests a degree of sadism or masochism.

Passenger - See Journey

People in dreams
People, particularly in dreams of a sexual nature, can be categorised in three different ways. The first is, as already briefly mentioned in the introduction, according to the archetypes. This is the essential balance between the masculine and feminine parts of our personality.

With sexual behaviour specifically in mind, the concept of the feminine archetypes can be widened to include the following:-

Kindly Mother - This is the traditional picture of the caring mother figure, forgiving flaws and always understanding. Until recently it was very easy to overdevelop this aspect at the expense of other sides of the personality, though now, through feminism, many women are aware of the problems which such stereotyping can cause.

Destructive Mother Often it is this aspect which either actively prevents or - because of the dreamer's relationship with his or her own mother - causes difficulty in other relationships. The problem is then exacerbated because such a woman will have learnt her way of operating from her own mother, and will know no different. This woman may be the 'smother-mother' type who is afraid to give her children their freedom, or the destructive, inhibiting mother.

Princess This is the fun-loving, innocent child-like aspect of femininity which is first and foremost spontaneous, but at the same time has a very subjective approach to other people. Sexually she may be quite fickle, partly because she needs a playmate rather than a partner. In her undeveloped state she needs to know that she can make demands on everyone around her, and that those demands will be met.

Siren This type is the seduc-

PEOPLE IN DREAMS

tress, primarily sexually and sensually aware, who has a strong sense of her own importance. She will be conscious of her own needs, although ultimately will have the ability to introduce the male to his own power. In dreams she often appears in historic, flowing garments as though to highlight the erotic image.

Amazon The amazon is the self sufficient-woman who feels she does not need the male and often becomes the career woman. She enjoys the cut and thrust of intellectual sparring. She is often a strategist, and in sexual terms will, when she does decide she needs a mate, plan her campaign down to the very last detail.

Competitor She is the woman who competes with everyone - both men and women - in an attempt to prove that she is able to control her own life. She will either frighten men off, or becomes the type of woman who, with panache, 'eats men for breakfast'.

Priestess This woman is totally at home within the inner world but often seems remote and untouchable from a sexual point of view. This is the highly sensitive woman who has learnt to control the flow of intuitive information and use it to enhance the world around her. Her passion is the link with universal truth.

Witch The intuitive woman who uses her energy to attain her own perceived ends is also feared for her seemingly magical qualities. She is usually subjective in her judgement and therefore tends to lose her discernment.

The masculine archetypes are:-

Kindly Father This aspect of the masculine is the conventional kindly father figure who is capable of looking after the child in his partner, but equally of being firm and fair. In many ways he is available to be experimented with, but ultimately is not hugely successful as a sexual partner.

The Ogre This represents the angry, overbearing, aggressive and frightening masculine figure. Often this image has arisen because the original relationship the dreamer had with their father - or father figure - was unsatisfactory. As a sexual partner he is very difficult since he tends to be very controlling.

Youth The fun loving, curious aspect of the masculine is both sensitive and creative. This is the 'Peter Pan' figure who has

PEOPLE IN DREAMS

never grown up. As a sexual partner he is unsatisfactory in that he can, like the princess, be over-demanding or unreliable.

Tramp This is the real freedom lover, the wanderer, the gypsy. He owes no allegiance to anyone and is interested only in what lies around the next corner. He often appears in dreams as the 'love them and leave them' type.

Hero The hero is the man who has elected to undertake his own journey of exploration. He is able to consider options and decide his next move. Often he appears as the Messianic figure in dreams. He will rescue the damsel in distress, but only as part of his own growth process. Women are most often attracted by this type - the knight in shining armour - but are disappointed when the romanticism wears off.

Villain The villain is completely selfishly involved, not caring whom he tramples on in his own search. He is often the aspect of masculinity women first meet in everyday relationships, so can remain in dream images as a threatening figure if she has not come to terms with his selfishness. The villain and the sorcerer can be confused sexually by a woman, but the villain is more selfish than dispassionate.

Priest The intuitive man is the one who recognises and understands the power of his own intuition, but who usually uses it in the services of his god or gods. He may appear in dreams as the Shaman or Pagan priest. He is often seen as sexually unapproachable, although there is an aspect of worship in any union made with him.

Sorcerer This is the man who uses discernment in a totally dispassionate way for neither good nor evil, but simply because he enjoys the use of power. In his more negative aspect he is the Trickster or Master of unexpected change. Sexually, he can be seen as dangerous, since union with him arises out of his dispassionate need to fulfil whatever he sees as necessary.

All of these personalities can appear in various guises in dreams as potential sexual partners. No-one is absolutely true to type and most people are a mixture of several. Spiritually, when we have access to all the archetypes, we are ready to become integrated and whole.

Characters in dreams
The second way in which peo-

PEOPLE IN DREAMS

ple can be categorised is by the roles they actually play in our dreams, and what these suggest. The people who appear in dreams are the characters with which we write our ' play.' Often we have a relationship with them in the here and now and they appear simply as themselves. We may introduce them in order to highlight a specific quality or characteristic. We may also permit them into our dream scenario as projections of our inner life or state of being.

In order to disentangle the various kinds of information which each character brings to the dreamer, it is often necessary to decide what or who each one makes us think of. That way we will reveal the deeper meanings and connections. Thus:-

A lover from the past could link us with that period of our lives, and with specific memories which may, or may not, be painful. Dreaming of **somebody else's mother, father, brother etc.** arises from the fact that sometimes we will not allow ourselves to feel emotions - such as jealousy - about our own family members. Displacement happens to disguise our feeling about our own family members.

Composite characters (characteristics from two people combined) Every character who appears in our dreams is a reflection of a facet or part of our own personality. This can often be better understood if we put ourselves in that person's position. To have a composite character appear in dreams of a sexual nature suggests that we have ambivalent feelings about ourselves and our conduct. Conversely in dreams there may be a noted difference between two of the participants, to illustrate two sides of the dreamer's thoughts and feelings. There may also be a marked contrast in the way the dreamer handles a situation with two of his dream characters. It is as though two options are being practised. One of these options may be more logical, the other more intuitively based.

Stages of growth can be highlighted in dreams - as can people's working activities - in order to emphasise the information given. In dreams with a sexual content certain characteristics highlight potential sexual behaviour.

Adolescent The emotions associated with adolescence are very natural and innocent and

PEOPLE IN DREAMS

such emotions may only be accessible through dreams. To dream of **being adolescent** focuses on the less developed side of oneself. The dreamer may be concerned over freedom of action in waking life. An **adolescent of the opposite sex** appearing in a dream usually means we will have to deal with a suppressed part of our personality.

Baby (Also see Individual Entry) To dream about a **baby that is our own** indicates that we need to recognise those insecurities - particularly sexual ones - over which we have no control. Psychologically we are in touch with the innocent curious side of ourselves, with that part which neither wants, nor needs, responsibility. If the **baby is someone else's** in the dream a woman may be coming to terms with issues connected with motherhood, and a man with issues of responsibility.

Boy If the **boy is known** he reflects recognised qualities in the dreamer and shows the potential for growth and new experience. To have a dream about a boy suggests that we are capable of contacting our natural drives and instincts.

Boyfriend To dream of a boyfriend, **whether present or former**, connects with the feelings, attachments and sexuality connected with him. Thought may need to be given to the loving, nurturing side of masculinity.

Child A child appearing in a dream usually represents the 'inner child'. **Beating a child** is reputed to represent masturbation.

Cripple (Also see Dwarf) A cripple in dreams can suggest someone who is emasculated, or fears of castration.

Carers such as nurses, nuns etc. Often the more compassionate, nurturing side of ourselves which has a vocation is perceived as the carer. Usually such women are beyond reach and therefore suggest a non-sexual relationship for a man.

Dwarf (or any grotesque gnomelike figure) Dreaming of a dwarf usually shows there is excessive pressure from the unconscious for the dreamer to recognise - and come to terms with - his thwarted sexual cravings and instincts. The penis is also symbolised by the dwarf.

Girl The qualities of intuition and perception may be somewhat undeveloped but can be made available to the dreamer. When a girl of any age appears in our dreams we are usually

PEOPLE IN DREAMS

attempting to make contact with our more sensitive, innocent side.

Girlfriend There may be fears to do with sexuality when a girlfriend or ex-girlfriend appears **in a man's dream.** If a girlfriend appears **in a woman's dream,** there can either be a concern about her in the dreamer's mind, or she (the dreamer) needs to search for - and find - qualities belonging to the friend in her.

Hero (or any heroic figure) In a man's dream the figure of the hero can represent all that is good in him. It does not normally represent the sexually active part. **In a woman's dream** he will suggest the Animus. **When the hero is on a quest, such as rescuing the maiden** part of ourselves which is at this time unconscious is driving us to find out what our limitations are. Our eventual integration still needs the challenge of the negative. **The death of the hero** can often suggest the need to develop the more intuitive side of ourselves, to be born again to something new. A **conflict between the hero and any other dream character** suggests that two facets of our own personality are at odds. The hero often appears in dreams to counterbalance a mistrusted person within the dreamer's everyday life.

An Inadequate person In the dream state, where we are safe, we may find it easier to confront our own inadequacies. Often a sense of sexual inadequacy or incompetence appears in dreams as an inadequate character.

King A king appearing in a dream represents the father or father-figure. When **the king is old or on the point of dying** the dreamer will be able to reject outworn or old-fashioned family values, particularly sexual attitudes. Some of the father's attitudes are alien to the dreamer, but should perhaps be accepted, if a personality such as **an emperor** appears.

Man Each of us has a repertoire of behaviours, some of which are acceptable and some of which are not. Any man appearing in a dream shows an aspect or facet of the dreamer's character in a recognisable form. In dreams those behaviours and characteristics can be magnified so that they are easily identified, often as personalities. Thus, **a sexually active man** in dreams would highlight our own sexual behaviour. A **man in a woman's dream** signifies the more logical side of her nature which enables

PEOPLE IN DREAMS

her to develop all the aspects of the masculine which allow her to function with success in the external world. She may be trying to understand her relationship with him if the **man is one she knows or loves**. **An unknown man** is generally that part of the dreamer's personality which is not recognised.

Pirate Dreaming of a pirate suggests there is an aspect of the dreamer's personality which destroys our emotional connection with the soul. In sexual terms it is someone who steals that which is not offered. This could be a girl's virginity, or her self-esteem.

Prince (Hero) and Princess As the Hero has taken responsibility for his own journey, so the prince and princess take responsibility for the lives they live. In a sexual sense they are the young, free and single aspect of us.

Queen The queen in dreams usually symbolises the dreamer's relationship with his or her mother, and thus with women in authority generally.

Twins (including the mirror-image of a figure in the dream) Twins in a dream can suggest two sides of our personality. If the **twins are identical** we may be recognising our ambiguous feelings about ourselves. **If not identical** they suggest the inner self and the outer reality. **Woman in a woman's dream** A woman is often representative of an aspect of her own personality, but frequently one she has not yet fully understood. **In a man's dream** such a figure may show how he relates to his female partner. **Oriental women** appearing in dreams usually suggest the mysterious side of the feminine. **In a man's dream** such a figure will often reveal his attitude to sexuality, while **in a woman's dream** it will reveal more about her own intuitive transcendent powers. **An older woman** mostly represents the dreamer's mother and her sense of inherited wisdom. **An unknown woman** in dreams will represent, in either a man or a woman, the unknown side of the personality. It is the quality of surprise and intrigue which allows us to explore further what relevance that figure may have. We can gain a great deal of information precisely because the figure is unknown.

Family

The third way in which we learn about ourselves in dreams is through our connections with our family.

PEOPLE IN DREAMS

Ideally, the search for individuality needs to take place within the family unit. Most of the conflicts and problems in life are experienced first of all within the family. In times of stress in adult life we will often dream of previous family problems and difficulties. In dreams we are able to manipulate the images of our family members so that we can work through those problems. In the journey towards individuality, dreaming of a parent's death can indicate that it may be time to break away from the family and to begin forming proper relationships, both sexual and otherwise, with other people. Arguments with parents often suggest that a change of attitude is needed by the dreamer towards family beliefs and customs.

Individual members of the family are often used by the dreaming self to highlight aspects of the dreamer's personality.

Brother In dreams a brother can represent rivalry and kinship. **For a man**, a brother can represent experience and authority and also vulnerability. **For a woman**, a brother can suggest her more masculine side, but also her need to take care of men around her.

Daughter When a daughter appears **in a man's dream** she will very often represent his fears, particularly those to do with sexuality, but also those to do with his relationship with his wife. **In a woman's dream** the daughter usually represents mutual support and understanding.

Extended family Members of the extended family, such as cousins, aunts, uncles, etc., often appear in dreams which have a sexual content in order to highlight particular qualities which the dreamer needs to recognise and integrate. (See dream about uncle in chapter on Deviations.)

Father In waking life the father is a role model. (For **a man** he represents how to be masculine, and for **a woman** how she initially perceives her ideal partner.) In dreams, particularly of a sexual content, father represents authority and moral rightness. He often signifies the personal authority which we adopt in relationships.

Husband/Wife/Live-in-partner Our self-image is very much influenced by our relationship with our partner. Our sexuality is very often dependent on the feedback we receive from them, and intimacy of body, mind and spirit is necessary within successful relationships. In dreams, the ways in which our partners appear to treat us can often highlight what we think of ourselves. Intimate one-to-one relationships form the cornerstone of our ability to relate to people outside our immediate family circle.

Mother The mother appearing in dreams represents **for a man** the bedrock of his relationship with other women. **For a woman**, such a dream highlights her own ability to be a mother. It is important to understand one's parents' sexuality in order to understand one's own.

Sister In dreams, the sister represents the feeling side of ourselves. Whether male or female, we need to make links with that side in order to create successful sexual relationships. Dreaming of having sex with one's sister, as with one's brother, simply suggests the need for integration of that part of our personality.

Son The son signifies the dreamer's need for self-expression. In sexual dreams, this figure can suggest parental responsibility.

In dreams with a sexual content it is worthwhile looking at an interpretation from all three points of view so that the best explanation can be used and understood.

Perversion - Also see chapter on Deviations

When a dreamer is not able to handle normal relationships and close bonding there may be dreams of perversion. These may range from bizarre acts that would not be normal in the dreamer's waking life to behaviour which is actively disapproved of by the society in which he lives.

Phallus

The image of the phallus and its many representations, such as the totem pole or the needle, is always to do with masculinity, creativity, and fertility.

Pine Cone

If the pine cone does not have a personal connection for the dreamer - such as a childhood memory - it will stand for fertility and good fortune. The shape of the pine cone and the fact that it contains many seeds gives an obvious connection to the phallus and masculinity. It can also signify the wish for orgiastic behaviour and a celebration of life.

Piston

Any machine appearing in dreams signifies mechanical action, or a rhythmic activity, so a piston can easily be seen to represent sexual drive and activity. Since the action is perceived as mechanical rather than tender it may highlight a lack of love. **In a woman's dream** a piston may demonstrate her fear of being hurt, both emotionally and otherwise. **In a man's dream** the piston may suggest virility and power. If the **piston is not rigid**, this may suggest a lack of desire or a fear of impotence.

Playing

Playing in dreams, particularly those of a sexual nature, will often represent foreplay and sometimes masturbation.

Ploughing

While the activity of ploughing is no longer very relevant in ordinary everyday life, in dreams it can still suggest fertility and fruitfulness. Planting of seeds obviously has sexual connotations, as also does the furrow. This is partly because of its appearance, and its resemblance to the female genitalia, but also because of a deeper symbolism of Mother Earth.

Prostitute

Often, dreaming of a prostitute forces us to look at our own sense of guilt or uncertainty about ourselves. It may also highlight a sexual need. **To be paying a prostitute** may suggest that the dreamer does not trust his own sexual abilities. **In a man's dream** it may signify his need for relationship at any cost. **In a woman's dream** it can suggest her own need for sexual freedom. Or she may be aware that she is prostituting herself in some other way - perhaps in the work situation. **To be being paid** for the sexual act may suggest that the dreamer does not feel valued as a person within a relationship.

Pulling

There are situations where we may feel pulled in more than one direction at once. This may be because of conflicting demands or desires. In dreams this can be shown by being physically pulled. In slang terms, pulling means picking up a potential partner. In dreams this can actually suggest our ability to be attractive to the opposite sex.

Q

Queen - Also see People in dreams
In slang terms, a queen represents a homosexual male and through wordplay may appear in dreams. A queen is also an authority figure and can therefore represent the mother or mother figure.

R

Rabbit
The idea that rabbits breed with exceptional fertility means that in dreams there is a connection with masculine ejaculation. At the same time the rabbit has the symbolism - like the hare - of being a representation of the mother.

Rain
Rain in **a woman's dream** can suggest the sexual act. It can also suggest certain forms of sexual activity which are seen to be fun.

Raincoat
A raincoat in a dream has obvious connections with sexuality, because of the image of the dirty mac. Oddly enough, it can also have connections with the womb, possibly because of the protective aspect against the elements.

Rape - See chapter on Deviations

Red
The colour red in dreams almost always signifies anger and passion.

Ring
Any ring appearing in a dream signifies wholeness and completion. A **wedding ring** signifies a successful relationship whereas **an engagement ring** might suggest a potential relationship, or more properly a relationship with potential.

Road - See Journey

Robe
A robe of any sort suggests a period of rest and relaxation. There are occasions when the mind rejects the idea of nudity being appropriate and will present us with the proper alternatives. If, for instance, in dreams the **robe is open** this could suggest an honesty of approach. A **dirty robe** would suggest that we need to consider our own

ROCKET

attitude to sex. The **colour of the robe** may indicate the type of response that is necessary; for instance a red robe would indicate passion, whereas a blue one would indicate coolness.

Rocket
The rocket - like the torpedo - is taken as a symbol of the phallus and of masculine virility. Its explosiveness is a symbol of ejaculation, so the two aspects put together signify the sexual act. Obviously a **rocket which does not fire** can suggest impotence.

S

Saddle
A saddle in dreams will suggest some form of sexual control, if there are other sexual symbols in the dream. For **a woman** this may suggest a particular way of acting, while for **a man**, he may need to be more conscious of his sexual drive and masculinity.

Sadism - Also see chapter on Deviations
Sadism is the wish to hurt or provoke a reaction - often in someone we love. In waking life most of us are not capable of being sadistic, but in dreams any action is acceptable. The very fact that actions are sadistic may also mean that they are masochistic as well - that is self-involved, and therefore in some way punishing oneself.

Salmon
In common with most fish when they appear in dreams, the salmon signifies our basic urges. It is phallic and signifies abundance and masculinity, although a salmon can appear in **a woman's dream** as a symbol of her wish for pregnancy. In its fight to mate by swimming upstream it also symbolises the sperm.

Screw
There tends to be an element of wordplay here. If a screw actually appears in a dream there may be some connection with the slang word used to suggest the sexual act.

Seed
In a woman's dream, depending on the other circumstances in the dream, a seed may suggest pregnancy. **In a man's dream** seed can highlight his thoughts and feelings on fertility.

Semen
In dreams semen may repre-

sent the life-force, and our perception of masculinity.

Sex
Each of us wants to be capable of supporting and loving at least one other human being. The sexual drive becomes an expression of this and we need our lover to be completely open both with us and to us. When a person's identity is dependent on partnership there will be difficulty with self-esteem and our sense of identity. Isolation can therefore give us problems. It is only when we learn that we do not need other people although we may want their companionship and their love that sex and sexuality becomes the correct expression of who we are.

Sexually Transmitted Diseases - Also see Venereal Disease
Dreaming of sexually transmitted diseases links with the human being's basic fear of being contaminated by sexual activity. Such activity puts us at both emotional and physical risk and the dreaming self sees this as the possibility of 'disease' rather than unease. In waking life the dreamer often perceives him or her self as being given something that they do not want - in dreams this manifests as a sexually transmitted disease.

Example
I dreamt I was at an STD clinic. The nurse asked me how I had caught the disease, but I couldn't answer. She said I would have to go into isolation to be de-contaminated.

This dream suggests that the dreamer is aware that he/she would be better off alone, rather than being in a relationship. The 'nurse' in the dream represents the part of the dreamer that is capable of healing a problem. Not knowing how the disease was contracted suggests a lack of clarity within relationships.

Shot, shooting - Also see Gun and Weapons
In a woman's dream being shot can symbolise the sexual act. Her feelings are involved, and she may feel that she is a victim or target. **In a man's dream** being shot can suggest that he is injured by his feelings for someone else.

Silver
In dreams, silver represents the feminine and gold the masculine.

Siren

The siren or temptress is such a deeply held image within a man's psyche that she will appear in dreams over and over again until he understands her. In mythological terms the hero must escape from the temptress in order to enter the real world, while the siren must relinquish her power over the male in order to allow him to be himself. In dreams where there is a strong sexual element, a woman needs to consider her seductive powers, whereas a man must consider his ability to be seduced.

Sowing

The image of sowing is obviously connected with fertility and fruitfulness, and can therefore suggest the sexual act.

Spear

The spear, in common with all pointed objects, is phallic and therefore represents the masculine. Because of its association with the warrior, it signifies aggressiveness and dominance.

Sprinkle/Sprinkling

Psychologically we need to make a link with our creative side in order to function properly as human beings. Dreams of sprinkling suggests the symbolism of impregnation, of conception and gestation. In more primitive cultures the semen was sprinkled on the earth in order to ensure fertility and good harvests.

Stab - Also see Knife and Weapons

Since a stab wound is penetrative, it obviously has connections with aggressive masculine sexuality, but also with the idea of breaking the hymen, and with virginity.

Statues

Statues appearing in dreams signify objects which should be worshipped and idolised. Often the **statue of a woman** suggests the mother or mother figure, but as someone who the dreamer does not see in a vibrant manner; almost an inert power. When the dreamer falls in love, a part of him or herself comes to life and this may be symbolised in dreams by **a statue coming to life**. **People turning to stone, figures that are made of stone but still move** Something which has previously been alive, e.g. a relationship, now is no longer valid in its old form.

Sterilise

When a **woman dreams of being sterilised**, she may be connecting with her feeling of powerlessness either as a woman or a mother. To dream of **sterilising something** suggests a need for cleansing at a deep level. We wish to get rid of hurts or traumas and are prepared to put in the effort to do so. **In a man's dream** sterilisation may suggest sexual dissatisfactions or doubts about his self-image.

Swimming

Swimming fish can have the same symbolism as sperm, and therefore the desire for a child. Swimming in water will always be symbolic of the emotions. Therefore to be **having difficulty swimming** would indicate that we are having problems dealing with an emotional situation in our lives; to be **swimming with ease** would show that we are coping well with emotional events around us. To be **swimming underwater** implies we should not get too emotionally involved in circumstances around us in our waking lives.

T

Tadpole - Also see Frog

Particularly in **a woman's dream** tadpoles symbolise the sperm, because of their shape, and may represent her wish to become pregnant. The tadpole can also represent the very basic sexual drive which we all have.

Tail

The tail can represent sexual excitement and, obviously, the penis. It can equally be accepted as those habits and behaviours we have inherited from our ancestors. The basic urges and drives that we have arise from our connection with the animal kingdom, and often images occur which take us right back to basics.

Tame

Sometimes in dreams the feelings we experience do not have the impact we expect. We may find them tame. This can suggest that our conscious appreciation of a sexual relationship can be greater than the reality. Conversely, if in dreams we are **taming an animal** we may be developing a

TEMPTATION

relationship with ourselves that allows us to satisfactorily move on to relationships with others.

Temptation
In dreams we can experience feelings and temptations we would not necessarily give way to in waking life. To experience **sexual temptation** may alert us to the fact that the relationships we have with members of the opposite sex may not be as secure as we first thought. Equally, to **meet temptation and to overcome it**, or rather not to yield to temptation, may make us aware that we are able to deal with our inner selves in a more gentle way.

Thirst
Often any need in dreams can arise from an unsatisfied requirement. This need may be sexual in origin, but presents itself in a hidden form in order to make more impact. We may want more emotional satisfaction, and should make some adjustments to the way we handle relationships.

Thorn
A thorn, being a sharp pointed object, often represents the sexual act or sometimes in women a fear of intercourse. In this sense, if the **thorn draws blood,** the act symbolises the taking of a virgin. This symbolism is seen in myths and fairy tales such as the tale of Sleeping Beauty, who is not awakened to her own power until the thorn is removed, when she is kissed.

Thread
A spool of thread suggests an ordered existence, and links to the old symbolism of the weaver of life (The spindle with the thread around it signified life itself). It is a symbol of everything which is feminine. **Threading a needle** thus has an obvious sexual reference and **having difficulty doing so** can also suggest some kind of sexual difficulty.

Toilet
Nowadays the toilet appearing in dreams suggests a need for privacy, and our ability to deal with our own needs and feelings in private. It will for many people have an association with sex and sexuality, and how we feel about ourselves. A **blocked toilet** might, for instance, suggest that our ability to express ourselves properly is impaired. To dream of going to **an unfamiliar toilet** suggests that we

may not have any idea what attitudes our partner or new relationship has to sex. Dreaming of **cleaning a toilet**, particularly if we realise it is not our own, suggests that we are capable of losing old beliefs and patterns of behaviour.

Tools

Dreaming of tools can suggest that we are questioning our own competence in some way. **Not being able to use tools properly** is a relatively common teenage dream, and the tool which is being used may be relevant. A **drill or screwdriver** might suggest the act of penetration, whereas a **hammer** could imply the 'pumping' action used in the sexual act. A **wood plane,** in taking off consecutive layers, signifies the act of defloration. The dreamer should be able to interpret the symbols as they appear.

Torpedo

A torpedo is obviously a phallic symbol, but is also a symbol of aggression. So, in dreams which contain a sexual element, the interpretation is one of aggressive sexuality. However, since a torpedo is fired only once - and thus destroys itself - its appearance in a dream can indicate a fear of sex or of premature ejaculation.

Touch

Touch is such an important part of intimacy, that how we deal with it in dreams can reveal a great deal about our own attitudes. We make contact through touch, and through pleasure. Often dreams about touching are the first indication we have about possible intimacy with someone else, or that our own attitude to touching or being touched is changing. Touch can also be healing, and many dreams about being touched are of this nature.

Tower

The tower is a very basic phallic symbol and as such will often appear in dreams. Equally, however, it can appear as a symbol of our own defensiveness and isolation from the world. To be **exploring the tower** suggests trying to come to terms with these guarded aspects of ourselves, and being able to move into a more comfortable position.

Toy

When **cuddly toys** appear in dreams we are in need of love and comfort. When there are more sexually explicit play-

TRANSFORMATION

things such as **sex toys** we are both attempting to move into more 'fun' elements within ourselves, and also using the symbolism of these things as being fantasy objects. Rather than being able to deal with reality in the appropriate way, we choose to use adult recreation.

Transformation

Any transformation occurring in a dream indicates that we are moving from one state of awareness to another. For instance, an **animal changing into a person** might suggest a change in attitude. One **place changing to another**, particularly if one of the places is known to us, indicates that there are probably feelings and emotions which need to be looked at. We all go through various stages of transformation in our waking lives, such as those from childhood to puberty, and from puberty to sexual maturity. These changes are often reflected in dreams.

Tunnel

The tunnel symbolises the birth canal and in dreams often reflects our own birth process. It also suggests our passage from basic instinctive drives to a more sophisticated awareness of our own abilities. This image often appears at times of great change.

U

Umbilical cord

In dreams the umbilical cord signifies the attachment that we make with people when forming relationships. In particular, not only our physical connection but also our emotional one with our mother, often has to be severed in order for us to make proper relationships with other people.

Undressing

To be undressing in a dream suggests a need for openness and honesty. We are attempting to put ourselves in touch with our own sexual feelings, or with those of other people. To be **watching someone else undressing** - rather than being a Peeping Tom activity - may be an attempt to come to a basic understanding of that person's emotional state. In waking life we may use this activity as a means of arousal. To be **undressing someone** in a dream suggests that we are aware of our own need for very close relationship which may or may not be sexual.

Vaccination

Vaccination can have the same meaning as injection and indicate sexual intercourse.

Vagina - Also see Body

Not many people dream directly of the vagina itself. It is usually represented or symbolised in some way - such as by a dark passage - or one of the symbols connected with femininity. Dreaming of one indicates that we are aware of the bodily processes to do with sex and sexuality, rather than the emotional ones.

V

Vampire

Because the human being's fear of the unknown is very elementary, ancient symbols that have represented this fear can still appear in dreams. Often the fear of emotional and sexual relationships can be portrayed in dreams and fantasies as a vampire. The succubus and incubus which preys on young people's vital or sexual energy is often pictured as a vampire. Such a symbol will appear in dreams as a warning to the dreamer that he needs to understand his sexuality better.

Vase

It is accepted that any hollow receptacle will represent the feminine in a dream. Usually it suggests the acceptive, receptive nature of woman. To **put flowers in a vase** suggests the sexual act, particularly if the dreamer is a woman.

Vault

Sexual potency or the unconscious is often represented in dreams by any dark, hidden place. A vault can also represent our store of personal resources, those things we have learnt as we grow and mature. To be **going down into a vault** represents our need to explore those areas of ourselves, particularly our sexuality, that have become hidden. We may also need to explore our attitude to death, since in many people's minds death and sex are closely linked through fear.

Venereal Disease - Also see Sexually Transmitted Diseases

To dream of **suffering from venereal disease** suggests that our attitude to sexual matters creates a problem for us. We may feel that we are contaminated in some way; for instance, our self-image has become distorted. Perhaps someone else's opinion of sex is 'infecting' us in a way that is harmful. Dreaming of VD can also suggest that other people may suffer from the same problems that we do.

Victim
In dreams when we sense that we are a victim, we are registering our powerlessness or passivity. Dreams of rape, burglary or incest (see Individual Entries) highlight the fact that we can continually put ourselves in 'no-win' situations. Although we may dream of this type of intrusion, while the image is sexual the cause of the dream may be emotional.

Virgin
The virginal mind - that is, a mind that is free from trickery and deceit - is perhaps more important than physically being a virgin. It is this aspect which often becomes evident in dreams with a sexual content. **In a woman's dream** such a figure suggests she is in touch with her own inner being. To dream of **being a virgin** suggests the woman's awareness of a state of innocence and purity. **In a man's dream to be having sex with a virgin** can mean that he needs to understand his own sexual identity and needs. He may need to feel the satisfaction of 'original conquest' of a woman. Dreaming of **someone else being a virgin** would suggest that our ideals of integrity and honesty are slightly separate from our own identity.

Volcano
An **erupting volcano** in a dream suggests that our emotions and passions are fairly explosive. The passion may well be uncontrollable, and sexually indicates the need for release and relief. An **extinct volcano** suggests that passions have died down and are now no longer active.

Vow
Making marriage vows in a dream suggests we are ready to make some type of commitment to another person. We may not necessarily in waking life be ready for marriage, but are ready to create relationships and partnerships. Making a vow is more earnest than a simple promise, and suggests that we are ready to take responsibility both for our own lives and someone else's. At the same time we trust that others are going to help us to keep our vows.

W

Wand
The influence which we have over others can often be of a sexual nature and is symbolised in dreams by a wand. This can also suggest sexual magic.

Want
When we become aware of our wants and desires in dreams, particularly when those desires are for a particular person, we are linking with our own basic nature. Often such wants are considered to be wrong and inappropriate, but in fact they are simply our way of coming to terms with something which is lacking in our lives. Often our dream selves will alert us to that lack, or to the fact that we have suppressed those physical and sexual needs, before we have brought that knowledge through into waking life.

Warmth
A feeling of warmth in a dream can give expression to the sense of well-being and fulfilment which comes from real and unconditional love. Warmth enhances our sense of comfort and well-being, particularly when in dreams we allow ourselves to be aware of others' warm feelings towards us. Psychologically, feelings of cheerfulness and hopefulness can create an awareness of warmth.

Watching
The part of us in a dream which watches and evaluates what is going on is that part which monitors our behaviour. Often sexual activity in a dream is entirely appropriate, and yet it is as though we can only accept it as a separate part of ourselves. We therefore seem to be watching the activity as much as taking part. When someone is **watching an erotic activity** in a dream, it can suggest coming to terms with their own sexuality.

Water
Many images connected with water have a hidden sexual implication. This is because emotion is so closely linked to sex and sexual activity that the two become interchangeable. Water represents the emotional, and therefore more feminine, side of the personality. Water - particularly for those who have not come to terms with their sexuality - can sug-

gest the need for cleanliness in sexual matters. It can also represent the idea of purity and innocence. Dreaming of **bathing with someone** suggests the need for intimacy. **Canals** in sexual dreams and fantasies can symbolise the feminine genitalia, and therefore the sexual act. **Drowning and floods** represent the chaotic side of us which can be uncontrollable and passionate. If the dreamer is afraid this can show that they are afraid of their passionate nature. **Fountains** suggest womanhood and all that is associated with the feminine.

Waterfall
A waterfall at its most basic level of interpretation can be taken to represent an orgasm. It can also signify any display of emotion that is forceful and yet somewhat controlled. Whenever any emotion reaches the stage where it must 'spill over' in order to become manageable it can be represented as a waterfall in dreams. In dreams with a homosexual element in them it can suggest what are called water sports.

Weapons
Most weapons traditionally represent male sexuality. For **a woman to dream of being shot** often indicates her wish for, or fear of, sexual aggression. If the dreamer is **using the weapon** he or she may be using their masculine abilities in quite an aggressive way, in order to defend themselves. In dreams any weapon has the symbolism of the action required to make it operational in waking life. Thus the hammer suggests using force in a situation, while the screwdriver is easily interpreted.

Wedding - See Marriage

Wedding Ring
Traditionally, the wedding ring was a symbol of total encircling love. **Losing one's wedding ring** symbolises a problem of denial within a marriage. It may be that there is a lack of commitment to loyalty and sexual faithfulness. To dream of **finding a wedding ring** suggests that we may be considering a relationship which requires us to make a promise to our partner, which is a promise of fidelity.

Whip/Lash
The whip is an instrument of torture and punishment. For this to appear in sexual dreams indicates the dreamer either

has the need to control others, or to be controlled by them. There are likely to be sadistic or masochistic tendencies in the dreamer which may or may not be overt. These tendencies may be the suppressed side of the dreamer's personality.

Wild
In dreams anything wild always represents the untamed. Often, because sexual behaviour has a wildness about it, wild behaviour in a dream can signify uncontrolled passion.

Worm
The worm can suggest the penis in sexual dreams. When the worm is not necessarily seen to be particularly clean there may be a sense of threat, depending on the dreamer's attitude to sexuality and gender.

Y

Yearn
Feelings in dreams are often heightened in their intensity. A need which may be perfectly manageable in ordinary everyday life becomes a yearning and seeking in dreams. To yearn for someone in a sexual way would suggest that we recognise a basic need for closeness and companionship. It may be that we have suppressed such needs through long habit or self-denial. An urgency may emerge in dreams for the very thing we have consciously denied. Such a dream would highlight an emotion which we may need to look at in order to understand.

Yield
Yielding is one of the more feminine attributes and signifies our need to let go and simply 'go with the flow'.

Yin-Yang
This symbol, as the balance of two complementary opposites, signifies a state of dynamic potential. In dreams it indicates the balance between the instinctive, intuitive nature of the feminine and the active, rational nature of the masculine. Ideally, perfect balance is created between two complementary opposites.

SECTION THREE
Dream Interpretation

Sex is symbolised in many dreams but when it appears directly, it shows we are more easily able to accept our own sexual urges and hurts. Our sex dreams show us what new challenges are being met and what growth is occurring. The only time our psychological and sexual natures stand still in development is when a pain or problem crystallises them at a particular level of maturity. Then the dreaming self presents the problem over and over again until it becomes solvable.

Any dream in which sexual images occur can be interpreted in a number of ways. The dreamer is left freedom of choice as to the correct interpretation for himself. It will depend which images were the most striking for him. Not all images in a dream dealing with sexuality are necessarily representations of the sexual act. They can often suggest how the dreamer handles his or her own sexuality, relationships and emotions. Dreams are obviously a very personal and private activity. If we believe that they also help us to sort out our impressions and information, they can often be a representation of assistance we may need in handling these issues in ourselves and others. Sexual dreams can also enable us to come to terms with aspects of ourselves which have caused us problems previously.

The most basic interpretation is to do with how one perceives oneself to be, and what one's sexual and sensual needs are. The second looks more at motivations and learning within a sexual dream, while the third interpretation is a much more internal appraisal of the balance between masculinity and femininity within oneself.

An illustration of how this works is:-

The dreamer is a 45-year-old mother of three, whose children are almost ready to leave home.

Example
I dreamt I was having sex with Lord Byron behind my mother's settee.

Interpretation one
The dreamer feels that her mother would not approve of her sexual activities, and that this activity must therefore remain hidden. She is prepared to take a risk, however, if it is romantic/important enough. Because the parental home often represents childhood, she is aware that she must come to terms with childhood perceptions and challenges before she can move on. In her case, her attitude to sex and sexuality must not hold her children back.

Interpretation two
There are two symbols of unconventionality here - Lord Byron and having sex behind the settee. A famous figure in dreams often means that we are seeking those qualities which we believe that person to have. In this case, not only is Byron a poet and therefore romantic, but his status as an aristocrat is also recognised. It is perhaps that by having sex in this way, the dreamer preserves the romantic mysterious side of herself, but also achieves status in her own eyes for having done so. The dreamer is aware of her traditional upbringing but also wishes to be more unconventional. She also wishes to be separate from her mother, while being aware of mother's impact on her own perceptions. She is prepared to accept responsibility for her own relationships, but is also being made aware of something lacking in her own life.

Interpretation three
The dreamer is recognising - and beginning to integrate within herself - the more romantic but misunderstood side of her personality (Lord Byron) in circumstances where she is both safe and at risk. This aspect of romanticism is masculine and sensitive rather than feminine and dreamy. There is a part of herself which she realises does not approve of the actions she is taking (the mother). She is mildly threatened by the potential for discovery and disapproval, but is also somewhat protected because the action is in a private situation where she cannot be seen unless she is searched for. She is looking for ways of protecting her own personal space, and of expressing herself somewhat unconventionally (This is the type of dream that a teenager may well have. In this case it is appropriate, since the dreamer did not have the opportunity to work these issues through during her own teenage years).

DREAMS

To help readers interpret their own dreams, included below are some interpretations of varying kinds of sexually orientated dreams by a representative cross-section of society.

The dreamer is 36-year-old heterosexual female. Her husband was 3 years younger than her. She and her husband divorced after 10 years of marriage, following an affair he had with another woman.

Example
I was in the foyer of a large building, which was quite modern and up-to-date. I was very upset by the fact that I had lost my handbag, which I knew had my passport in it. I kept asking people if they had seen or found it. They either replied negatively, ignored me or kept pointing further and further into the building.

Interpretation one
The large building is this lady's new life and suggests she needs to be more modern and up-to-date. She feels she has lost both her femininity (the bag) and her identity (her passport). She is appealing for help from people outside herself who cannot or will not help her but are pointing her into being more and more depressed or introverted.

Interpretation two
Because she is in the foyer of the building, she is at the start of something new. She is going to have to cope with situations which may be very different from those she normally encounters. She is upset by what has happened, since her right to her own identity has been taken away from her by the loss of everything that she values. She is looking for reassurance and information from other people, which she cannot have, although, because a building usually represents the self, she will eventually be able to find what she needs within herself.

Interpretation three
Any building in dreams can represent the way we feel about ourselves, so the dreamer is aware that she can still be modern and up-to-date in her perception of herself. At the same time she has suffered a great deal because her identity and her right to be recognised has been taken away from her. This is borne out by the

fact that other people seem to be ignoring what has happened, and equally ignoring her distress. Without the confirmation of her own femininity she is not functioning properly. This is demonstrated by the loss of the bag, and also by the people being unable to help her. People in dreams often represent other aspects of our own personality. Though at present she is a 'helpless female', ultimately her interaction with other people will help her to explore those aspects of herself that at the moment are frightening (the recesses of the building) which will enable her to find the answer. This may necessitate her exploring her own depths for the answers.

The dreamer is a 30-year-old homosexual male.

Example
I was with my partner. We were in a settlement - not a town, but not a village either. We went up a very steep hill which looked like a forest. On the hill there were 'discarded' railway carriages. Some of them had been turned into homes illegally. I felt they were being squatted rather than being properly inhabited. Some of the carriages were rusty and had not been put to any use and I went inside a couple of them. I was hoping for a sexual encounter inside the dark carriages. It was as though actually entering the carriages had a strongly sexual connotation. No sexual encounter took place.

My partner and I continued to the top of the hill, where there was a wonderful view. We saw two trains going along a very steep, narrow track down the hill. I got the feeling that it was for this reason we were going up the hill. There were already some other people waiting for the trains. One of these people was wondering if these trains were going to make it down the hill, or if they would tumble down.
In the distance we saw the two trains arriving. The first was rather old-looking - possibly a steam train - and it was followed, very closely, by a second one which looked like a road coach on train wheels. It was much bigger than the first and had large tinted windows, although I could still see the passengers inside.

The trains then started going down the hill. The second larger train got stuck in a bend temporarily. The trains then carried on down the hill, along the very narrow track which was bordered by trees which seemed to have lots of branches.

Interpretation one
This dream can be interpreted in three different sections.
Looking for a sexual encounter is seen as normal, since the dreamer is a gay man. The darkened carriages signify the hidden side of himself, and he is aware of the risk involved in entering these 'illegal' homes. (The carriages are not being used for their original purpose, and have been taken over to be used as homes.) It would seem that the homes are temporary resting places. There is an erotic charge in looking for sex, if not in the sexual act itself.
In the next part of the dream, the dreamer and his partner are overcoming obstacles of which other people are also aware. Reaching the top of the hill through a forest (representing the feminine), they are then waiting for something to happen. The two trains in fact represent the dreamer and his partner, and there is some doubt as to whether they can succeed.
In the third part of the dream the trains represent both the past and the future, and also the differing attitudes held by the dreamer and his partner. There is a temporary hitch in that the larger coach - probably the dreamer - gets held up. Their onward path is protected by life itself (the trees), but also there is a further connection with the feminine more sensitive side of the dreamer himself.

Interpretation two
The dreamer becomes aware through this dream of the very strong links between himself and his partner. They have certain difficulties to be overcome, both inherent in their lifestyle (the settlement itself), and what goes on within that lifestyle. Sexual activity and the opportunity for such activity is exciting in itself, but is not available if the relationship is to succeed. There is some doubt in the dreamer's mind as to his own motivations for seeking sex elsewhere (the darkened carriages) though it is perfectly natural to do so. The way they are going to go forward needs to be carefully considered in view of past experience, and the dreamer is aware of changes in his own perception of himself. These may cause difficulties in their joint way forward, although this can be overcome through his own sensitivity and intuition.

Interpretation three
Spiritually the dreamer is aware that he must move through the customs and beliefs within his own lifestyle. He must overcome the obstacles within himself (both the mountain and the carriages) in order to reach the best in himself. Only when he has done this can proper consideration be given to the best way forward for him and

his partner (the trains). He has to realise that part of the relationship and old ways of behaving are becoming outworn, although just because he has found a new way of being (the modern carriage), it does not mean that the old ways are not still valid.

The dreamer is a 34-year-old lesbian.

Example
I was driving in a car in the countryside with my ex-boyfriend. The car broke down and we started arguing. I ran away and jumped over a big stone wall. I then found myself in a park where there was a black panther. It leapt up and, as I warded it off, it bit me on the wrist.

Interpretation one
Although on the face of it this dream is not sexually orientated, it is evident that it is about relationships. There is a breakdown in this relationship (the car), which causes arguments. The dreamer wishes to escape from this and jumps a barrier (the wall), which puts her in a different space. A park in dreams often has the same significance as a meadow, which signifies the feminine side of our natures. The panther - through its association with cats - suggests a very strong sensual, sensuous part of the dreamer. In biting the dreamer, this 'negative' is working against her.

Interpretation two
While knowing herself to be lesbian, the dreamer had previously had a long relationship with her boyfriend which had been mainly focused on her supporting him on an emotional level. The countryside here suggests idyllic surroundings which are being passed by. There is no further motivation to continue the relationship and there are arguments and a breakdown. The dreamer wishes to run away but is actually crossing a dividing line within herself into a more structured life (the lesbian lifestyle). The panther is the wilder, more free side of her personality which, if not checked, will give her problems (being bitten is often seen as a return to a vulnerable more baby like state).

Interpretation three
The dreamer is attempting to integrate both the masculine and feminine sides of her personality. There is conflict which she is trying to avoid but to do this she must overcome a barrier within herself and enter a more structured female environment (represent-

ed by the park). Even within this there is a wilder destructive side to her nature which will 'bite back' at her if she is not careful.

The dreamer is a 28-year-old heterosexual female. She had the dream about six months after splitting up, quite acrimoniously, from her boyfriend after a relationship lasting two and a half years. They resumed a friendship several weeks later.

Example
It was a bright summer's day. I was at either a car boot or jumble sale. I looked behind me and saw a large (about 3 ft long) lime-green snake with large black eyes and black spots covering its head and going part way down its back. I was frightened of it and tried going underneath one of the tables to escape from it, but it followed me. I then climbed on the table and was running very fast. The snake was still following me. I looked back at it and realised that I need not be afraid of it any longer.

Interpretation one
The snake symbolises sexuality, and in common dream interpretation the colour of lime green signifies loyalty. The black spots suggest negativity, so this whole dream is about sexual loyalty and the dreamer's fears connected with this. In following her, the snake (her sexuality) is drawing attention to itself. It is initially frightening and something to escape from, although later she is prepared to accept it as a valid part of her life.

Interpretation two
The setting of the dream is important, since it suggests getting rid of old things (jumble sale). The snake representing sexual loyalty is frightening, but although the dreamer tries to hide, it is an issue that she needs to deal with. It is something which must be brought out into the open (the tables) and dealt with speedily in order for the dreamer to lose her fears, otherwise the problem will simply pursue her.

Interpretation three
There is confusion in the dreamer's mind as to whether what she has is valuable or not. She is being troubled by her own doubts and fears, particularly issues to do with both her own and her partner's loyalty to one another. She is doing her best to escape from those doubts. Through the dream she realises she cannot avoid the issues of sex and loyalty, no matter how hard she tries to escape.

She does not, however, necessarily have to confront the issues, since - simply by the action of actually trying to escape and then finding that she is no longer afraid - she deals with the problem.

The dreamer of the following 2 dreams is a 30-year-old heterosexual male actor.
At the time of the first dream he was 15 or 16. Even at that time he had ambitions to be an actor.

Example
I was watching television alone. A programme came on featuring a famous male pop star who at the time was thought by many people to be female. I felt strongly sexually and emotionally attracted to 'her', and wanted to get to know her as a friend as well as a lover.

In waking life, I found out several weeks later that 'she' was a 'he'. I was very disappointed to discover this, yet still felt some attraction and was unable to comprehend this. I was unable to discuss this with my friends.

Interpretation one
This dream is fairly typical of a teenage dream, and is an attempt to sort out the dreamer's perceptions of masculinity and femininity and hence his own sexuality. There is so-called puppy-love; additionally, the object of his affections is unavailable to him because 'she' (by appearing on television and not in person) is unattainable. The dreamer is aware of his own needs for friendship and love, which arise out of his being alone in the dream.

Interpretation two
In being alone the young man has an opportunity to consider aspects of his own sensitivity, as well as his own ambitions (represented by the 'female' pop star). He can do this objectively (suggested by the image of the television), but he is also aware of his own sexual and emotional needs. He wants to understand his own personality, and his unconscious self has given him an image of someone who appears to be a role model. His disappointment and reactions in waking life suggest that he is not attracted to men, but finds the masculine/feminine balance interesting.

Interpretation three
At about the age of fifteen to sixteen there is inevitably some confusion between two different urges or drives. One is the urge

towards expressing one's sexuality correctly, and the other is expressing one's creativity appropriately. This dream brings both of these issues together to be considered. The boy finds the pop star erotically attractive, but also wishes to get to know and understand 'her' (and therefore himself) better. 'She' represents the balance between his own creativity and sexuality in a way that he can easily understand, and places the two issues in a context where they can be jointly expressed. The television programme gives him this framework in which to work. On some level he also recognises that only he can reconcile the two aspects of himself. By being alone he can also be objective about this.

At the time of this dream the dreamer was 29 years old, and in a stable relationship with a younger woman.

Example
I was in a room with the male lead singer - who is known to be bisexual - of a well-known band. He is about 10 years older than me. In waking life I admire him. We were standing up talking and I was facing him. Although I did not feel threatened, I decided to leave. It was at this point that I noticed he was naked from the waist down. The singer did not want me to leave and although he was not aggressive towards me, he was expecting some sort of sexual activity to take place. I appreciated that it was a misunderstanding and felt no malice towards him, although I felt relieved at being able to leave.

Interpretation one
In this dream there is still an awareness of the masculine/feminine balance (bisexuality) and an admiration, presumably of the way the singer is. The dreamer decides to leave, even although the singer (that part of the dreamer which is sensitive and creative) is made vulnerable by this. The creative aspect recognises the need for some kind of union within the personality, though this is denied in the dream. The dreamer feels more in control of his own actions, and is not disturbed by the vulnerability.

Interpretation two
The dreamer is aware of his own ambitions and aspirations, but now sees them in a more sensible light. The combination of sensitivity and drive in him can make him very vulnerable and perhaps needy. (All characters in dreams are parts of ourselves.) He is able to walk away from that part of himself, recognising that his assumptions about himself are no longer valid, and that he can

develop other successful relationships. His sexuality and sensitivity are no longer an issue which will help or hinder his career.

Interpretation three
Taken in context with the first dream, the dreamer is sorting out the issues he has to do with performance, whether this is sexual or theatre. He is confident enough in his own being to walk away from a situation where his vulnerability becomes apparent, because he recognises the conclusions he came to at a young age, where the two seemed to be linked, are no longer valid.

The dreamer is a 32 year old single mother of 2 children. She was brought up mainly by her father and aunt.
The first dream demonstrates how a child's early experience can have an effect on her perception of men, and how they are going to treat her. For some time in adult life, she experienced emotional and physical conflict within her sexual relationships.

Example
This dream took place when I was 6 or 7 and involved the house I lived in at the time. It was a two-storey house which also had a basement. We lived on the top floor.

In the dream the sea was across the road. I was looking at out at it when the sea became angry and started lapping against the window. A man who was covered in shingle and seaweed was in the sea and kept banging against the window whilst asking me to open the window so he could come and get me.

Interpretation one
This dream illustrates very fully the type of nightmare that children can have when they are trying to sort out problems of authority and masculinity and femininity. The sea represents the emotions, and the child recognises that she may be overcome by the 'sea'. The man represents her view of 'father figure', who is himself in a highly emotional state, but cannot reach her. While she is safe inside the house for the moment, she is also aware that she is vulnerable. She also instinctively recognises that in allowing the man to pass through the barrier between them (the window) she is in danger.

Interpretation two
The sea, which represents the heightened emotion that is going on round about her at the time, is not 'hers' in that it is across the

road. However, the problems associated with these emotions are getting worse and are beginning to get at her. The man covered in seaweed and shingle represents the way her father appears to her in his own emotional difficulties. She understand that she can be sucked into the problems around her.

Interpretation three
The most frightening thing to a child is when she is not in control. While relatively safe within the confines of her own room, she nevertheless recognises the difficulties that are occurring around her. Her own inner feelings are welling up and giving her problems. The man appearing from the sea is a classical representation of the god Neptune - or Poseidon - who rules over storms and earthquakes. While he appears harmful to her, and frightening because she does not understand, ultimately he is father figure and therefore helpful.

This dream occurred when the dreamer was about 30 years old. In waking life she is now involved with a man whose character is much kinder and more sympathetic than any of her previous relationships.

Example
I was in a riot. I could hear lots of shouting and glass was breaking all around me. I was hiding in the stairwell of a building with a female neighbour of mine, who is older than me. I was absolutely petrified. I knew that the building was not one involved in the riot.

When it went quiet we walked down the stairs to where the police were, but the woman who was with me was now my sister. The police led my sister and I to safety along with the other residents of the block. We had to go down 7 steps which were covered in silver glass. The policeman told us to take care as we were going down. When we reached the bottom, my sister asked me where I was going. I told her I was going home to my boyfriend (We do not live together in waking life). I woke up and was not at all frightened.

Interpretation one
In waking life, this lady is used to anger and difficulty and having to handle angry people. This dream reveals her real fear behind having to deal with such problems. While being scared she also recognises that she is not involved in that anger (represented by the building she is in). Once the difficulties have passed, she is able to refer to a higher authority (the police) who help her to get

away from the difficulties. By being prepared to go carefully away from the situation, the dreamer recognises the sanctuary that her boyfriend represents.

Interpretation two
The number seven is significant in this dream since there are seven stages of development as the child grows to maturity. The anxiety and fear that the dreamer has felt in the past, and which she recognises keeps her in a continual state of tension, can now be left behind. Glass is used symbolically twice here; firstly in the breaking glass signifying old facades and barriers being broken down, and secondly as a representation of the clear path and steps forward that she must take toward safety. It is as though she must back-track to a state of innocence (by going down the stairs) before she can make a decision as to what she must do. Her sister's question alerts her to the fact that she is now safe with her boyfriend.

Interpretation three
The three aspects of the feminine in this dream - the sister, the older friend and the dreamer herself - suggest the three attitudes the dreamer has towards femininity. While she is distressed by the riot she is also protected by the older friend, who in this case would represent wisdom. When the difficulty has died down the older friend then changes into the sister - a more intimate side of herself. She is then, having made contact with this aspect of herself, able to move away from conflict. Helped by her own authority - the police - with care, she can rediscover her own femininity by going down into her own inner self (the steps) which reinforce the femininity and the clarity (represented by the silver and glass). She then knows what is the right thing to do and is prepared to trust her boyfriend.

The following dream is significant in highlighting how the dreamer has succeeded in integrating her knowledge about herself.

I was in a room talking/arguing with a girl I did not know. I was wearing a skirt, she was wearing trousers and a flying jacket. She grabbed my arms; as she did this I hit her over the head with a beer bottle. I hit her from left to right, which is not a natural movement for me as I am right-handed.

Interpretation
The dreamer recognises the conflict between her own more femi-

nine side (herself wearing a skirt) and her more masculinised side (trousers and flying jacket). This latter side is trying to restrict her, but the dreamer is in control since she uses a symbol of masculinity (the beer bottle), which is also accepted as feminine (a hollow container). She hits from left to right - which is accepted as being from the feminine side to the masculine. It is significant that the dreamer recognises this, since previously she has had to act in a very strong 'masculine' way.

The dreamer is a 38-year-old heterosexual male.

Example
I was with a girl, we were both naked standing up, and going to kiss. The surroundings were unclear, but we were alone. As I approached to hold her, she opened her mouth and showed her tongue to kiss. As we touched and kissed, other tongues - long tongues - appeared from every orifice in her body - her eyes, ears, nostrils, vagina - and all over her body. They moved rapidly and voraciously over my body, holding me tightly to her and licking me all over, covering me in her saliva. Her arms became unnecessary as her tongues held me close and increasingly tightened myself to her. It was as if she would have eaten, or drowned me, but I didn't resist, we didn't make love, or touch other than within the embrace. We were locked together tightly, and no attempt was made by either of us to get away. It was a very pleasurable encounter and something I was happy to submit to.

Interpretation one
Being naked here suggests the dreamer is vulnerable. The girl is open to sexual intercourse. Revealing her tongue signifies this and the appearance of the tongues - which are often taken to suggest the phallus - signifies that her approach is all-consuming. There is no need for the dreamer to be held by her arms since he is already enthralled by her approach. The point of the dream is that the dreamer was not repulsed by such an embrace, but was happy to submit to being 'devoured'.

Interpretation two
Nakedness can represent openness and innocence. As stated elsewhere in the book, men are very fearful of being consumed by their women. The dreamer appears to have lost this fear, and therefore is coming to terms with the sexually voracious and seductive side of his partner. He is aware that he can be eaten or

DREAM INTERPRETATION

drowned, which suggests that he is also in touch with his partner's emotional self. Her tongues (the way she expresses herself) are sufficient to hold the dreamer, and it appears that this is sufficient for him, since no actual intercourse took place.

Interpretation three
The long tongues with their similarity to snakes suggests a connection to Medusa, the destroyer of men. In mythology the only way that she could be beheaded was by looking at her image in a mirror. The dreamer, however, seems content to confront his partner's destructiveness face to face. In this, he is confronting his own inner feminine and recognising that he can be held by it and not destroyed.

Example
A girl and I were alone and naked, the surroundings were unclear, but unimportant. We were close, but not making love, just content to be alone. Flying ants descended on us - it is not clear if there were two large ants, or many small flying ants, but they picked us up and flew us to a secluded paradise and left us there, alone and happy.

Interpretation one
Here the dreamer is aware of the contentment that there is in partnership. The only thing that can make the situation better is by being transported to paradise. This is done by allowing the perception of the lower sexual urges (represented by the ants) to be enhanced.

Interpretation two
Most of this dream seems to be unclear. It appears to concentrate on the dreamer's need to be alone with his partner to enhance their enjoyment.

Interpretation three
The dreamer is apparently aware of the spiritual content of the sexual act. While he and his partner are initially alone, the ants assist him in creating bliss for himself and his partner.

The dreamer is a 27 year old heterosexual female.

Example
I dreamt I was looking out of a window and I saw a huge bear clawing over a fence at a collie dog. As they both went for each other, with the dog's owners looking on, the two animals were electrocuted by the fence. The dog wrapped itself around the fence, and

was caught up in it, the bear just froze, falling backwards. The owners of the dog pulled it off the fence. This process meant the dog's legs fell off, they eventually untangled it, and lay with the dog on the ground, exhausted & weeping. I ran downstairs to tell my friends what I had seen from the window.

Interpretation one
This dream is interesting in that it uses symbolism throughout. There is conflict here between the masculine and the feminine (the dog and the bear). The energy which is created by the barriers which they put up will destroy them both. It will render the bear impotent (frozen) and will emasculate the dog (its legs falling off).

Interpretation two
The owners of the dog do not seem to be prepared to take responsibility for it until it has been harmed. The dog appears to have destroyed itself in wrapping itself around the fence (the barrier), which would seem to indicate a self-destructive streak. The dreamer herself seems to be separated from the action by the window, but also seems to have a need to share what has happened with her friends. Only when a real mess has been created do the owners become emotionally involved.

Interpretation three
The dreamer does not seem to be able to sort out what is going on in her own life. There are difficulties being created, which can only be resolved through conflict. There can only be a lose - lose situation, in that the bear becomes powerless and the dog loses its life. Neither do the owners gain anything by waiting until the conflict is over.

The dreamer is a woman in her late thirties, who is trying to balance her needs between career and partnership.

Example
I was walking on a beach, at first alone, and then met a man I didn't know. We had to build a sand-castle, and then I knew we would have sex. When I looked at the sand-castle it was in the shape of a computer.

Interpretation one
The dreamer is quite happy to be a woman on her own (symbolised by the beach), but is attracted to her new friend. The sand, however, suggests that the relationship would not be a permanent

DREAM INTERPRETATION

one. The computer signifies that her career is important to her, but at this stage also feels impermanent.

Interpretation two
At this point in her career the dreamer cannot decide whether she wants a permanent relationship or not. She appears to be aware that she is in need of a relationship of some sort, (having to build a sandcastle), but it would have to be shaped by the demands of her career.

Interpretation three
The dreamer appreciates that she does not particularly know what her motivations are (the man) but is aware that she needs some fun in her life. She is ambivalent about having pleasure outside the work environment.

The dreamer is a 15-year-old girl.

Example
I dreamt I was a young child playing on the beach with my father. He suddenly picked me up and started throwing me up in the air. My present boyfriend (who my parents do not like) was standing in the background. I asked my father to put me down, which he did. I then realised there was another man standing behind my boyfriend, and I 'knew' this was the person I would leave with.

Interpretation one
This young lady is aware that her father is still treating her as a child. Her boyfriend is not yet mature or strong enough to stand up to her father. She must therefore take control, but realises that her present boyfriend is not her ultimate partner.

Interpretation two
It is important to the dreamer that she is able to maintain the good relationship that she has with her father. Because her parents do not like her boyfriend she feels insecure (being thrown up in the air), but is aware of her own responsibility in this situation. Because of the interplay between the two men, she is able to recognise her own ideal partner.

Interpretation three
It is not until the dreamer has sorted out the conflict between her own childish needs and her more adult wishes that she is able to

form any idea of how she will handle relationships with the men in her life.

Postscript

This dreamer is a 39-year-old heterosexual female. This dream happened after she had been proof-reading part of this book.

The people who own the flat beneath me are getting married. In my dream they were living above me. I was lying in bed and realised that the pattern of their carpet (which was big swirly flowers) was coming through the ceiling. I then found myself in bed with the man (I am not attracted to him in waking life), and was prepared to have sex with him.

Interpretation one
The dreamer recognises her own need for married partnership, which she perhaps feels will give her status (living above). The flowers in the carpet represent her own femininity, of which she is becoming more aware. While she does not consciously fancy her neighbour, she is aware that he is the type of person she would like to marry.

Interpretation two
Her friends' marriage has made her more conscious of her own single state. She is aware that she needs to become more feminine, and to acknowledge that femininity as being a basic part of her personality. When she is prepared to acknowledge this a loving partnership will occur quite naturally.

Interpretation three
By recognising her own ability to be both friend and lover with a potential partner, she achieved recognition of herself as a woman.

Hopefully, many of my readers will gain new insights and information in the same way as this lady did.

Happy Dreaming!